Devon's Ancient
Bench Ends

Devon's Ancient Bench Ends

Todd Gray

Todd Gray

THE MINT PRESS

The Mint Press
Taddyforde House South,
Taddyforde Estate,
New North Road, Exeter EX4 4AT

© Todd Gray 2012

Text design and page make-up: Topics – The Creative Partnership, Exeter.
Cover design: Delphine Jones.
Printed and bound in Great Britain by Short Run Press, Exeter, England.

ISBN 978 1 903356 61 6

Craftmen's tools at Abbotsham

For Ivan and Tegwyn

*All photographs within this publication
have been taken by the author.*

Contents

Note & Acknowledgements

Each of Devon's ancient churches has been visited to assess whether they have surviving bench ends. I have defined Devon so as to include those parishes which were part of the Diocese of Exeter or County of Devon at the time of the Reformation such as Broadwoodwidger (transferred to the Archdeaconry of Cornwall from 1875 to about 1919), Churchstanton (transferred to the County of Somerset in 1896), Maker (transferred to the County of Cornwall in 1844), North Petherwin (transferred to the County of Cornwall in 1966), North Tamerton (part of which was in Devon until transferred to the County of Cornwall in 1844), Virginstow (transferred to Archdeaconry of Cornwall in 1875), and Thorncombe (transferred to the County of Dorset in 1844), Wambrook (transferred to the County of Somerset in 1896). Other parishes which have changed their status, such as Chardstock (in Dorset until transferred to the County of Devon in 1896), Dalwood (in Dorset until transferred to the County of Devon in 1844), Hawkchurch (in Dorset until transferred to the County of Devon in 1896) and Stockland (transferred to the County of Devon from Dorset in 1844) are not of direct interest to this study because they were not ancient Devon parishes. They also do not have relevant bench ends and do not feature in comparisons with the border parishes.[1] I have not included benches held by private individuals.

Devon's Ancient Bench Ends marks the culmination of an interest that began at East Budleigh's All Saints' Church in 1985 when, as a postgraduate student, I was introduced to Devon's bench ends. I was overwhelmed by the carving and intrigued by a discussion with Professor David Quinn on the 'Red Indian'. Four years later I was appointed a Research Fellow at Exeter University's then outpost in Cornwall and I extended that work to include researching maritime themes carved on Cornish bench ends. Several decades have passed and I finally feel able to finish what feels like a very long project although some considerable questions remain. During the course of these years I have accumulated many debts. I am deeply grateful to friends and colleagues with whom I have travelled more than ten thousand miles through every part of Devon, and into the three bordering counties, and would like to thank John Allan, David Cook, Carole & Ray Herbert, Meg Hitchcock, Martin & Rosemary Horrell, Laurence Hunt, David Kremer, Willow MacFarlan, Olive Millward, Richard Parker, Mark

Right: A figure at Powderham Castle Chapel.

Rowe, Carole Vivian, Rob Ward and Keith Stevens. This would have been an impossible task but for their time, interest and inevitable patience. More importantly, it has made it possible for this non-driver to visit, and often revisit, what are often remote churches. I have taken solace in remembering that illustrious figures such as W. G. Hoskins, Nikolaus Pevsner and Violet Pinwill were also limited to travelling as passengers and journeyed through the same lanes. It has not lessened my debt but has made me feel I am following the ghosts of others who were like-minded but similarly impaired. Churchwardens and officers have shared their knowledge and opened their churches to allow me access. I am very grateful to them for the many kindnesses they have shown. I am also indebted to the staff, too many to name individually, of the Cornwall Record Office, Devon Record Office, Exeter Cathedral Archive, North Devon Athenaeum, North Devon Record Office, Plymouth & West Devon Record Office, Plymouth Local Studies Library, Somerset Record Office, University of Exeter Main Library, Victoria & Albert Museum and Westcountry Studies Library. Margery Rowe, former Devon County Archivist, has without fail shared her extensive and invaluable knowledge of the county's archives. My Tuesday classes have provided

Left: Another of the bench end women at Powderham Castle Chapel.

listening ears to tentative examinations of my explorations into bench ends and given much appreciated encouragement. I would also like to thank Delphine Jones for once again providing a superb cover. Hugh Harrison has made me very much aware of considering the physical construction of the benches and to him I am very grateful. Professors Mark Brayshay, Julia Crick, Mark Stoyle and Alexandra Walsham, both colleagues and friends, have been generous in sharing their knowledge and expertise. Professor Martha Carlin, Dr Penny Hebgin-Barnes, Dr Eleanor Lowe and Dr Catherine Richardson have been kind in answering questions from a complete stranger. I am particularly grateful to Steve Hobbs for his insights from a much-appreciated Hartland perspective which has been particularly valuable to me given his knowledge both in the field and amongst the church's rich documents. John Allan and Richard Parker have also been generous in their time and in making invaluable suggestions in improving the text. They have saved me from innumerable blunders. Any and all mistakes are of course my own.

This book was published in part with the aid of a grant from *English Heritage* reflecting its value in supporting the *National Heritage Protection Plan*.

Taddyforde, Exeter, August 2012

Introduction

Two early writers have described Devon people during a Sunday service in their parish church. One was Philip Nichols who is thought to have been a witness to one of the best-known tales about Plymouth. He described the local reaction when Francis Drake suddenly returned from the West Indies in August 1573. Nichols wrote that the ship:

'arrived at Plymouth, on Sunday, about sermon time, August the ninth 1573. At what time, the news of our Captain's return brought unto this, did so speedily pass over all the church, and surpass their minds with desire and delight to see him, that very few or none remained with the Preacher, all hastening to see the evidence of God's love and blessing towards our Gracious Queen and Country, by the fruit of our Captain's labour and success.' [2]

Nichols, a chaplain, made no further comment on this behaviour nor did Drake, himself the son of a vicar. It provides no details on the interior of St Andrew's Church but fortunately an account for a different church has survived for the period before the Civil War. The author of *A True Relation of Those Sad and Lamentable*

Accidents Which Happened In and About the Parish Church of Withycombe in the Dartmoores in Devonshire on Sunday the 21 of October last 1638 was also not intent on illuminating Devonians in the midst of their weekly devotions but his pamphlet is full of detail. On that day the church was damaged during a particularly violent storm and he was concerned to describe that event as well as note the possible implications for the souls of the parishioners. On that morning the sky blackened, so much so that, according to the writer, the congregation could not see one another. Then suddenly the tower was struck by lightning. The pamphlet recorded that the parishioners:

'the most part of them fell down upon their knees, some on their faces and some one upon another with a great cry of scalding and burning, they all giving themselves up for dead, supposing the last judgement day had come, and that they had been in the very flames of hell.'

Left: *High Bickington.* **Right:** *The church as portrayed in the pamphlet.*

The pamphlet described the destruction and death as the lightning bolt coursed through the church. In the telling of the story the writer inadvertently provided details on how, in 1638, the church was filled with seats and hints at the social distinctions in where everyone sat. For example, he described the burning of the minister's wife:

'the lightning seized upon his poor wife, fired her ruff and linen next to her body, and her clothes, to the burning of many parts of her body in a very pitiful manner. And one Mistress Ditford sitting in the pew with the minister's wife was also much scalded but the maid and child sitting at the pew door had no harm.'

The lightning passed from the vicar to a man sitting nearby (*'his head was cloven, his skull rent into three pieces and his brains thrown upon the ground whole'*) and damaged the men who were sitting together with him. In these passages the pamphlet revealed that men and women sat in separate sections and that seats then had doors. In another section the writer indicated differences in seats for those with a high status.

'Master Hill, a gentleman of good account in the parish, sitting in his seat in the chancel, had his head suddenly smitten by the wall, through the violence whereof he died that night, no other hurt being found about his body. His son sitting in the same seat had no harm.' [3]

Another version noted that Hill and his son had a seat that only accommodated two persons. It also mentioned seats in the body of the church were upturned and that eight boys sitting around the communion table were unhurt. Finally, the report revealed that even funereal furniture was used to sit upon:

'One man, sitting upon the church bier, at the lower end, the bier was struck and torn, and he that sat thereon was thrown into one of the pews by the wall side.'

Although not concerned with doing so, the pamphlet shows not only that seats had been erected by that date but it indicates that villagers each had

do visitors pause to examine them. In this building is an extraordinary collection of benches: the eye's gaze is filled with rows of oak seats but nearly every one is too plain, unadorned and unassuming to be noticed. The vast majority of the more than 100 late medieval benches rarely cause a visitor to admire the ancient workmanship. It is true that seats in other churches are more attention-grabbing and have thus captured the imaginations of generations of visitors as well as members of congregations, but Devon has a variety of bench carvings that by their very nature complement all those others waiting to be discovered across the county. The seats at St Nectan's are, on the whole, elementary in design but

their own places determined by their individual circumstances.

The pamphlet is important in that it provides contemporary evidence in relation to one of the ways in which Devon is distinct from the rest of England. Its ancient church benches are among the most remarkable in the country in both their number and character of carving. Despite this, and the fact that seats occupy more space in a church than any other fitting, they are often unappreciated by the casual visitor who is more likely to look at stained glass, monuments and other more eye-catching features. The church of St Nectan at Hartland, for example, is a treasure house of ancient seats but rarely

Hartland.

13

they are also remarkable survivals of the work of Devon's early craftsmen. They form one part of a surprisingly fascinating facet of the past.

Devon's church seats take various forms: as elsewhere there are sedilia, choir stalls with misericords, benches, pews and chairs. Amongst them is a wealth of rare and unusual carved wood but their continued survival is threatened by the current fashion for replacing old seats. Their number and variety is being rapidly reduced. This cull is particularly noticeable with those seats installed in the mid to late 1800s. Devon is acknowledged on a national level for its ancient bench ends but what has yet to be appreciated is that it also has a rich legacy of high-quality Victorian and Edwardian

Simply carved bench ends at Coldridge.

carving. It is likely that many will be destroyed before it is realised how distinguished this woodwork is. In some Devon churches the seating is much-loved and carefully looked after but in others there is an indifference and apathy which does not bode well for their continued survival.

This lack of appreciation is partly due to the seats being largely unstudied despite nearly two hundred years having passed since two local clerics, in the 1820s, first brought them to the attention of the public. Only a generation passed, in the 1860s, before Exeter's Harry Hems had a very prosperous business built partly on restoring ancient benches and he established himself as one of the country's leading experts on church carving. It was not until the early 1900s that the most detailed work was being undertaken on these seats. The Misses Cresswell, Prideaux and Clarke,[4] three local ladies who must have had great determination, visited Devon's country churches by railway and horse and examined ancient woodwork with what was a limited use of photography. Shortly afterwards a national study appeared[5] but it would be another fifty years, in the mid to late 1900s, before work of a comparable standard would again be produced[6]. It is only in these first years of the new Millenium that interest has been revived and some exemplary work has been published.[7] There is a growing national interest in the history of church seats and it comes at this crucial moment in their

Late bench ends repositioned with earlier ones at Monkleigh.

development.[8] Despite nearly 200 years of interest this is the first study to look systematically at all Devon's ancient benches.

A quarter of the county's ancient churches retain ancient benches. No fewer than 123 of Devon's 464 surviving medieval churches[9] have between them some 2,500 ancient benches. It is partly for this number that Devon's benches are remarkable: they comprise a considerable portion of those that survive across the country. Devon is also notable for being part of a regional style. Westcountry bench ends tend to be rectangular and flat at their tops unlike those in East Anglia, the other part of England with a significant proportion of early bench ends, which is known for its poppy heads. It has yet to be determined why each region developed its own style but what will be demonstrated in the following pages is not only that Devon differs in its designs from other parts of the South West but also that that there are variations within the county. Devon had distinct traditions within what has long been recognised as a regional style.

One distinction is that there are unusual parish collections which stylistically have no parallels even

EXMOOR

Countisbury
Combe Martin
Mortehoe
Parracombe

Marwood

Braunton
Stoke Rivers
Ashford
Swimbridge
Westleigh
Tawstock
Horwood

Abbotsham
Bideford
West Anstey
Yarnscombe
George Nympton
Hartland
Clovelly
Alwington
Littleham
Landcross
Atherington
Warkleigh
Clayhanger
Weare Giffard
Satterleigh
Welcome
West Woolfardisworthy
Monkleigh
High Bickington
Huntsham
Frithelstock

Roborough
Churchstanton

Sutcombe
Newton St Petrock
Dolton
Cheldon

Dowland

DEVON
Puddington
Thornbury
Buckland Filleigh

West Worlington
Pancrasweek
Nymet Rowland
Lapford
Upton
Bickleigh
Hatherleigh
Bondleigh
Hellions
Stockleigh
Bridgerule
Northlew
Honeychurch
Coldridge
Down
Pomeroy
Cadbury
Plymtree
Payhembury
Tetcott
Inwardleigh
St Mary
Talaton
Feniton
Ashwater
North Tawton
Sandford
Shobrooke
Thorverton
Colebrooke
Crediton
Rewe
Whimple
Ottery St Mary
South Tawton
Cheriton Bishop
Stoke Canon
Northleigh
St Giles in the Heath
Broadwoodwidger
Drewsteignton
Tedburn St Mary
Pinhoe
Seaton
Lewtrenchard
Throwleigh
EXETER
Venn Ottery
Shillingford
Clyst St George
Lifton
Dunchideock
Kenn
Bridford
Kenton
Woodbury
Doddiscombsleigh
Ashton
Powderham
East Budleigh
North Bovey

DARTMOOR
Chudleigh
Ashcombe
Ilsington

Combe-in-Teignhead
East Ogwell
Tavistock
Torbryan
Broadhempston
Buckland Monachorum
Staverton
Cockington
Bere Ferrers
Dartington

Stoke Gabriel
Churston Ferrers
Plympton St Mary
PLYMOUTH
Modbury

Kingston

Kingsbridge

South Huish

Churches with Ancient Bench Ends

within Devon. Churches such as Ashcombe, Bideford, Bondleigh, Churchstanton, St Giles on the Heath, Tetcott and Whimple are among those that would appear to be unique. Judging by their designs, few craftsmen appear to have produced benches in more than one church. There are some exceptions. The plainness of Hartland appears to be similar with work at nearby Clovelly and another workman seems to have been at both Broadwoodwidger and Lewtrenchard. A distance of less than three miles lies between them. In each church there are three bench ends that appear to be duplicated. Motifs also suggest that the churchwardens employed this craftsman. The bench ends at Honeychurch are also like those at Nymet Rowland which lies only seven miles distant. Likewise, the close similarities between bench end designs suggests the individual who worked at Westleigh in North Devon also carved at Newton St Petrock. This is a greater distance, some eleven miles. There are also interesting comparisons between the carvings in the churches at Ottery St Mary and Seaton. Despite these examples, the vast majority of parish churches have bench ends in which it is difficult to show exact parallels in other buildings. It is much easier to find parish churches sharing craftsmen in the neighbouring counties of Cornwall and Somerset.

There is also an intriguing possibility of workmen carving in the North Devon church at Frithelstock and at the Cornish church of St Eval. Each has a bench end with a strikingly similar crown of thorns as well as a pair of

Carving at St Eval near Padstow in Cornwall.

Similar carving at Frithelstock in North Devon.

17

Modbury's pulpit.

Drewsteignton's single surviving bench end.

Opposite and page 20:
Examples of a style of carving at High Bickington.

two heads. Both churches are conveniently situated near a port (Bideford and Padstow) which would have made the 48 mile journey relatively easy. The bench ends also share a common carpenter's mark.

Many benches still serve their original purpose but there are some ends that have been deployed to embellish pulpits, reredoses and panelling. Some have even been reused in the entrance porches: at George Nympton they have been cut down, painted white and used to support new seats. The benches are scattered around the county and distributed unevenly: there are some churches such as Braunton which have dozens of seats and others are like Countisbury and Drewsteignton which have only one. Some collections dominate their churches but many are part of a patchwork of seating with a mix of high pews, later benches or chairs.

Devon's ancient bench ends range in colour from light grey to black. Age, exposure to the elements and treatment by oil, varnish or paint has given them very different visual characters. The warm honeyed tones at East Budleigh are sharply in contrast with the parched appearance of the seats at Honeychurch or with the dark sombre wood of Chudleigh's benches. Despite their variation in colour, it is likely they are all made of oak although for some time it was thought those at Braunton were of chestnut.[10] The timber is rarely specified in accounts. The Plympton St Mary carpenter who was commissioned in the 1490s by Bodmin acquired his oak from Wales, as did a Somerset bench end carver in the 1520s,[11] but just over a hundred years later, in 1601, the oak for Braunton's seats was noted as having come from the churchyard. It appears another oak tree was similarly cut down for seats in 1579. There was also a transportation cost for new seats in 1593 that shows other carving was done outside Braunton.[12] There is one documentary reference to timber being used which was not oak: in 1555 seats were made at Dartmouth St Saviours partly from 'bechin' and 'vyr' or 'ffyer', which was presumably beech and fir/pine.[13]

Many ancient benches display signs of age. Damage through damp is more noticeable at the base where it has risen through the floor. Wear and tear marks are often

on the vulnerable areas of the woodwork and the last fifty years have seen the introduction of marked lines, running about 6 to 12 inches from the base, caused by vacuum cleaners. Graffiti are also common particularly in those seats furthest from the pulpit or the gaze of churchwardens. The centuries of wear and tear make it easier to identify those that are ancient but some, like those at Mortehoe, are more difficult to distinguish from the Victorian ones.

There is little evidence for where the seats were made. The churchwardens' note at Braunton about transporting seats is rare. Another uncommon detail survives as part of the testimony of a craftsman in a Cornish part of the Exeter diocese in 1597. Gregory Venner of St Kew told the church court he made and later brought three seats to the church of St Tudy.[14]

Benches were probably not the first type of seat. It is often assumed that the earliest were made of stone and set around columns or walls. This premise is now being questioned.[15] One early seat was the form, the simple seat constructed of wooden planks with legs at each corner. It was relatively cheap to produce and was presumably portable. However, by the 1400s and, possibly earlier, fixed benches were being installed. These were similar to forms but offered greater comfort in that they also had backs and ends. In that Cornish part of the Exeter diocese in 1597 the seating was referred to as chairs[16] but in another Cornish parish it seems the word may not

have had the modern meaning: in the early 1600s one parishioner of Kenwyn described four particular 'chairs or pews', which covered an area of twelve feet by six feet, as having seated seventeen people.[17] These were more likely to be benches and not chairs as we know them. The only early chairs yet found in a Devon church are 'two framed chairs' which were in the Lady Chapel at Crediton on 27 May 1545.[18] Whether any transportable individual seats, chairs or stools, were ever brought into other Devon churches for the congregations at that time has not yet been determined. Pews, the high enclosed seats which gradually took the form of boxes, were in Devon by the early 1600s and became the dominant format for the following two hundred years.

The study of all these seats is hampered partly by the scarcity of written evidence. There are few churchwardens' accounts, the record which is most likely to record the parish erecting seats, for the years before 1500. Many seats were privately paid for and these appear in records mostly when there were disputes.[19] Only Dartmouth St Saviour's and Braunton's sixteenth-century churchwardens' accounts show substantial continual building of seats but even these show some seats were erected earlier. The accounts for Dartington and Chudleigh, which range from 1554 and 1566 onwards, do not record such sizeable expenditure. Dartington spent only twenty pence in 1556 for seating. In comparison, Chudleigh's parishioners paid 42 shillings and 4 pence in 1567 for the vicar's seat and some forms and then nine years later spent another 53 shillings and 4 pence for new seats. This was a sizeable amount but even so it was not enough to fill the church with oak benches.[20] The inference from the accounts is that if seats had been built at the expense of the parish then they were usually in place before the accounts began.

Other documents show seats elsewhere were installed in the early 1400s but this does not preclude there having been a yet earlier phase. Documents record seats were erected but not that they were the first ones in the church. References require careful use. For instance, in 1534 Morebath church was described as having been 'new seated'[21] but this could indicate either that existing seats were being replaced or that the church was first acquiring them. Likewise, an enquiry undertaken at West Ogwell into seating in 1613 provides other evidence. One parishioner, Thomas Stanckham, remembered the seats for 60 years and said his father had told him it had been seated at least for one hundred years previously.[22] There are no other documents to confirm or refute this claim. Without such evidence it is difficult to ascribe dates to most seats as any analysis of their styles is inconclusive.

Our understanding of seating is also limited by the patchy survival of the seats themselves, despite what is nationally a high survival rate in Devon, and the survivors may be unrepresentative of those that have been lost. There are many reasons for the loss. Churchwardens often complained in the seventeenth and eighteenth centuries that new seats were necessary because the existing ones were, in the example of Georgian Blackawton, 'ancient and useless' and 'too far decayed to be repaired'. Other church officials said their seats were 'all out of repair and decayed' (Cadeleigh, 1766) and so 'decayed and dilapidated' that they were no longer sufficient (Broadwoodkelly, 1825).[23] Wooden seats suffered from damp rising through the floors and such damage was compounded by those churches with insufficient planching, the wooden base on which

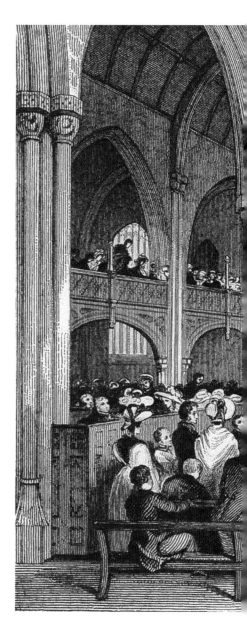

Engraving of St Andrew's Church, Plymouth, 1830, illustrating the variety of seating.

Sandford's Victorian seating with reused early bench ends.

seats were erected. It may have been because of this that in 1797 Reverend Richard Polwhele, one of Devon's early historians, noted Bridford's seats were 'old and rotten'.[24] A few years later the vicar wrote:

'I remember some very old and decayed benches with carved ends at the back of the rectory seats in the chancel. The upright end of one represented in bold relief the figure of an old woman in the very ancient dress of the English peasantry with the old long-waisted bodice and a broom elevated in her hand pursuing a fox who is seen making off with a plundered goose slung over his back with the neck firmly grasped by his jaws. These were so decayed as to defy attempts to restore them.'[25]

The seats were destroyed and what appears to have been good carving was lost because of decay as well as, arguably, indifference.

At least four other reasons can be ascribed to the change in seats. One is the issuing of official orders. The

24

reports of the rural deans demonstrate the influence they could wield in effecting change. For example, in 1781 Chivelstone's churchwardens informed the bishop that they had been instructed by the rural dean to erect new seats.[26] Perhaps the views of an individual were instrumental in changing furnishings throughout a deanery. This could account for why the South Hams is largely bereft of ancient benches.

A second reason for loss is that piecemeal installation seems to have eventually had the unintended consequence of destruction. Many seats were individually funded and sporadically erected, with the result that some churches progressively lacked uniformity in its seating. At Colyton for example, the churchwardens wanted new seats partly because of this piecemeal approach. They complained that the existing seats were not only *'very indecently kept'* but *'promiscuously and disorderly built'*.[27]

Another reason for change was unexpected calamity. In one parish, St Budeaux outside Plymouth, new seats were erected because the earlier ones had been destroyed during the Civil War.[28] No doubt this was also true of Great Torrington where the church was blown up during that war. German bombing in the Second World War also caused the destruction of seats in both Exeter and Plymouth as well as in a number of towns and several villages such as Clyst St George. It was not war but a fire at Exeter St Stephen's that caused new seats to be installed

in the 1660s[29] and lightning caused great damage at Cruwys Morchard which resulted in the church being re-seated in 1701.[30]

Finally, taste and fashion have played a major part in introducing change. This extended to all fittings throughout churches. One good example of this is the church of Harford where clerics noted changes in the parish register. In 1825 the rector, Robert Savage, wrote a memorandum that 'a figure of a female angel, holding a trumpet, was placed over the pulpit'. The angel was a gift from Savage and a successor, Reverend Sanders, subsequently wrote in 1854, 'this ridiculous figure, after having a wing, part of the trumpet and a leg broken off, was finally removed by the hands of a stranger'. In 1902 another cleric added 'the figure in question was probably in better taste than Mr Sanders' comment upon it'.[31]

The changes are particularly well-chronicled as congregations followed the gentry fashion for high enclosed pews. Curiously, in 1812 it was said of St Sidwell's Church in Exeter that a plan aimed to provide good accommodation with the ability to see and hear the minister clearly but also coolness was an objective.[32] A much more representative view was that enclosed seats were an improvement on benches: they provided privacy, were warmer and more clearly separated occupiers from their neighbours. The partition of parishioners was particularly important as it could help distinguish social status. In 1843 one Devon commentator caustically

A bench end at Newton St Petrock with the Renaissance figure common to North Devon.

remembered 'the more ambitious towns-folk would all be little squires and have box pews'.[33]

In the early 1800s fashion turned from high pews to embrace low benches. By the 1820s two Devon writers advocated retaining benches and derided the pews.[34] Within a generation the Exeter Diocesan Architectural Society was formed and it proved a valuable ally in promoting benches. By the middle of the nineteenth century the public had a greater awareness and appreciation of the old seats. Of the North Devon parish of Newton St Petrock it was said in 1884 that 'in the fitting up of the pulpit the architect has employed some very fine old carved oak which was apparently valued but little in former times it being found under the floor at the back of the seats. From this material, also, some fine carved oak bench ends were made.'[35] This, as will be discussed more fully in the pages below, was one of many parishes to restore and replace carved benches. A century ago Beatrix Cresswell, who would undoubtedly have heard many stories about changes in Devon's church fabric, also noted benches were reused, face down, as bases on which to erect new pews.[36] In many other cases the benches were just destroyed.

Whatever the reason for change, whether due to decay, official instruction, lack of uniformity, calamity or fashion, more than a hundred Devon churches retain at least one ancient seat and most have many more. They are most likely to be found in country churches whereas in contrast, no ancient bench ends survive *in situ* in city or town churches where urban populations were more likely to take up new styles and to have the funds to effect change.

The terminology used in Devon churches has evolved over the years. In the sixteenth and seventeenth century seats were often referred to as 'seidges', particularly in relation to the parish rate for seating.[37] This was derived from the Latin

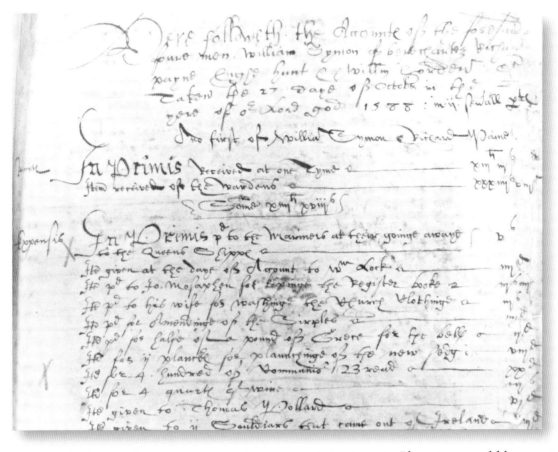

Churchwardens' account for Braunton, 1588, with an entry for the 'sedg'.

the correct term was often tutt. It appears as though the local pronunciation was tit.[38] In some places it was known as a butt; for example, at Buckland in the Moor in the 1640s and 1660s, the parish paid for a butt to kneel on and another for the communion table. Those who cleaned the church and showed people to pews were known in some local churches as butt-women. Thus, Ann Parkin, a seventy-four year-old butt-woman recorded in the census of 1891 as living in Plympton, would have put out the butts or tutts or tits as she walked along the alley leading from the loft.[39] In Hartland small stools were known as crickets.[40]

By the late sixteenth century there seems to have been an indiscriminate use of the words seat and pew. However, for the sake of convenience in trying to make the meaning clear, the word 'pew' is used in the following pages to describe a high seat boxed-in with a door and 'seat' is used as a generic term.

sedes for seat. Alley was used in preference to aisle through to at least the early nineteenth century. Lofts in Devon as elsewhere could mean a rood loft as well as what is known elsewhere as a gallery. What is described as a kneeler today was formerly known widely as a hassock but in southern England, and across Devon, including in Hartland from at least the 1630s onwards,

One of the carvings featuring a cow at High Bickington.

PART ONE

THE HISTORY OF SEATING

Seats for the clergy

The pre-eminent early seats in a parish church were not for the congregation but for the clergy. The most magnificent one in Devon is undoubtedly that of the bishop at Exeter Cathedral. This is hardly surprising given his superior status but its size has dwarfed every occupant for 700 years.

Likewise, in parish churches the most imposing ancient seats were also for clerics. The priest, and other clergy, had a set of seats, normally three and always made of stone, which can still be found in a small number of parish churches. These *sedilia* are normally built into the south wall of the sanctuary and can be highly decorated. Individually each seat

Left: Sutcombe.
Below: The seats for the clergy at West Ogwell.

is called a *sedile*, the Latin word for chair. More than two dozen ancient ones survive for Devon.[41]

The most impressive medieval *sedilla* are at Crediton and Ottery St Mary. That at Broadclyst was later converted to hold a medieval effigy. The seat reflected the hierarchy of the holders with the priest occupying the higher seat to the east. This can be seen at Branscombe and Plympton St Mary. West Ogwell has one which is particularly elegant. The need for them ceased when the Reformation simplified the liturgy and removed the roles of the deacons and sub deacons.[42] The Victorians restored some, such as at Paignton St John which was reconstructed in 1870 from fragments, and new ones were created.[43]

There are other early impressive seats: choir stalls were erected in chancels and can have elaborate carving in the misericord. Misericords take their name from the Latin word for mercy (*misericordiae)*, hence they have also been described as mercy or compassion seats. These are made of wood and tip up like a cinema seat to allow the occupant to partially rest his weight while remaining standing as needed during parts of the Mass and offices. Six Devon churches have preserved misericords, in total there are 22 examples, a third of the number at Exeter Cathedral which has the earliest collection in the country.[44] Those in the parish churches are nevertheless highly interesting. They all were installed before the Reformation.

The chief interest in them lies with the carved under-sides: there is a central image and sometimes lesser carvings, known as supporters, were on either side. The two at Atherington depict foliage. The ten at Ottery St Mary (in the chancel and the Lady Chapel) are either of a longhaired male head or of Bishop Grandisson's heraldic arms. The three at Bovey Tracey are more varied. One has foliage, a second is of a man with a forked beard and the third depicts a fox taking a goose. The supporters of each of the three misericords are birds.

Choir stall at Ottery St Mary with the misericords.

Cockington's two misericords are thought to have been removed from nearby Torre Abbey. One is of St Matthew flanked by angels and scrolls while the second is of a seated St Luke who is flanked by winged bulls. There are two at Kingsbridge which are part of a two-seat bench. The misericord on the right is blank while that on the left has a carved angel displaying a shield. The outside arm rests each have a finial of a robed and beheaded figure. Finally, Marwood has three choir stalls with foliate carvings.

These seats were not typical of parish churches. They were to be found in those churches which were served by colleges of clergy rather than by individual parish priests.

Misericord at Bovey Tracey of a fox.

Seats for the laity

It has long been suggested, as noted earlier, that the congregation's first seats were made of stone and placed along the edges of the nave but it may be that the earliest of all were less accomplished types of wooden furniture.

Left: Two of Abbotsham's shields with unusual carvings.
***Below:** A chicken at Marwood.*

The Lady Chapel at Crediton had, in 1545, stools amongst the other seats. More commonly identified in churches were forms, the backless benches on four legs. No ancient form appears to have survived. In the mid 1800s a visitor to Heanton Punchardon commented that the chancel was free of seating except for forms which 'for kneeling are placed according to immemorial local custom'.[45] Even earlier was the use of forms for sitting. One of the earliest that was recorded was one that stood before the organ in 1441 at Dartmouth St Saviour's and another was built in 1496 for the rector's clerk to sit on.[46] In 1597 the aforementioned note of chairs in a Cornish parish concerned a dispute over erecting new seats in St Tudy. The joiner built a bench in a place which he noted there were no chairs or pews but only, he said, a form.[47] In 1581 the property of the church at Braunton had included eight forms. Three had been used within the church.[48]

Forms were not exclusively for the poor. At Combe Martin in the 1570s and 1580s men paid for their wives to have the right to sit not on a bench but on a form. Others paid for what was described as seats in the aisle. These must have been forms as

35

well. This may seem late but in the early 1620s and 1630s the same payments were made: several men were still paying for their wives' places on forms. One was for a form in the north aisle, another was for one placed immediately in front of the pulpit and a third was located below the north door and presumably in the aisle.[49]

Another use was near the wooden communion table which had replaced the medieval stone altars. In 1573 forms were erected to place around the table at Crediton and five years later Woodbury had the same.[50]

The laity have seen five major phases of seating during the last six hundred years. The forms were probably displaced by medieval benches with backs which themselves were gradually overtaken in the first years of the seventeenth century by boxed-in pews which were in turn followed by a Victorian resurgence in reinstating benches and in installing chairs. The late twentieth century brought with it the insertion of moveable seats, some made of plastic, and most recently there has been a fashion for wooden benches and chairs which are moveable and thus flexible in regards to the use of floor space. One constant feature of the function of these seats is the desire for increasing comfort.

An example of Churchstanton's Gothic foliage set in a diaper pattern.

Benches

In 1287 a synod, at Exeter, discussed seating and ruled that no parishioner could claim priority for any seat except members of the nobility and patrons of the church.

Left: One of the unusual creatures at Frithelstock.
Below: An oddly constructed head with an abusurdly pointed chin at Abbotsham.

The discussion demonstrates a sufficient number of churches had seats and it showed that disputes over where parishioners sat was underway by this date.[51] How extensively churches were seated is unclear but by the fifteenth century churchwardens' accounts show seats had been installed. Some six centuries later the quarter of Devon's ancient churches that retain them have an unequal distribution. Broadhempston's single bench end is in contrast to the 94 at Braunton. Hartland has even more of the more than 2,500 ancient carved benches in the county.[52]

The earliest recorded seats were at Dartmouth: the first documentary reference is for 1438 when John Peirs paid for a seat. Other parishioners made similar payments through that century and those that followed. Many entries refer to men's wives being charged for their seats and there were seat repairs in 1496 and 1539.[53] During this time the seats at St Petrock's Church in Exeter were also mended. An agreement made on 14 February 1519 between the carpenters and the churchwardens stipulated seats in a new aisle would resemble the existing ones.[54] More than a generation earlier, in 1472, a seat had been erected in the church for the organist.[55] Plympton St Mary had seats by 1491. That year Matthew More, a carpenter, was contracted to erect similar seats at Bodmin.[56] These seats at Dartmouth, Plympton St Mary and Exeter St Petrock have not survived but there are several different styles of panels at Bodmin which could be those by More. In that church there are bench ends with Renaissance imagery and Gothic tracery including shields with images of the Passion. This is all of a high standard of carving.

Ashburton also had some of Devon's earliest recorded benches. The churchwardens' accounts show there were seats as early as 1484 and then twenty-seven years later, in 1511, John Mayne, apparently a local man, was paid to build additional seats. This continued for the next eight years. There were further charges for seating in 1522 when carvers were paid for the rood loft. In 1568 the parish erected additional seats for the clergy.[57] Chagford's church officers were repairing a seat in 1481 but recorded no particular expenditure on seats for the following two generations.[58] This could indicate that the church was already fully seated. Documentary evidence also shows seats were erected in such places as the church of Allhallows in Goldsmith Street in Exeter in 1550 and at Tavistock also during the reign of Edward VI.[59]

By 1495 the mayor of Plymouth had a seat in St Andrew's Church. His office would have required a symbolic high-status place for him to sit as well as additional items to highlight his importance: that year a carpet was purchased for him to sit upon

Carvings of the Passion at Bodmin in Cornwall.

and three years later cushions were decorated with the town arms. In 1509 a new seat, described as a pew, was made for the mayor which presumably indicates that the previous one was out-dated or no longer serviceable. Four years later, as before, the town purchased a cushion, made of carpet, for the mayor to sit upon.[60] It is not known if there were seats for the congregation.

The earliest surviving dated seat for a Devon parish church appears to be one of 1489 from Lifton. This is now at Launceston Museum.[61] Even earlier is the fragment of a choir stall at Exeter Cathedral which dates to the fourteenth century. Others from that set were reused at nearby St Laurence's Church and they survived until the Exeter Blitz of 1942.[62] There are eight benches in parish churches which were carved with sixteenth-century dates. These are at Broadwoodwidger (1529), Huntsham (1534), East Budleigh (1537), Northlew (1537), Dowland (1546), Alwington (1580), Dolton (1581) and a bench end at Landcross appears to indicate either the year 1503 or 1552 in Roman numerals.[63] Other benches have been given similar dates by their heraldry or, in the case of Hartland (1580) by initials or an inscription (Coldridge, 1511).

In 1635 Hartland parishioners claimed that there was an 'ancient custom' in apportioning seats: the implication of the statement 'beyond the memory of man' is that the seats were in place some considerable time before the late sixteenth century. They also claimed that the church retained ancient documents that provided details of the arrangements.[64] Churchwardens' accounts record 'the new pew' was built in 1557 and the inference is that there was already seating.

Increasing prosperity in Devon from the 1400s through to the sixteenth century no doubt accelerated the enhancement or even

Remnant of a Lifton bench end now in Launceston, Cornwall.

41

Broadwoodwidger.   *East Budleigh.*   *Northlew.*   *Alwington.*

provision of seats for the laity. It is unlikely that all the seats in one church were installed at the same time. Records show that in Braunton the churchwardens continued to build new benches at intervals from the 1550s through to the 1630s: seats were erected in 1557, 1560, 1568, 1578, 1579, 1583, 1588, 1593, 1607 and others in about 1635.[65] St Giles in the Wood also erected seats at different times in the late sixteenth century[66] as did Dartmouth St Saviour's.[67] It is likely that other Devon churches had their seats built over several years and by different individuals.

It has been speculated that seats in churches coincided with the building of church houses, a form of early church hall, because of the need to retain open spaces.[68] This argument is based on the assumption that seats were not in churches before the church houses. The growth of seating has also been linked to the Protestant emphasis on sermon-giving with the notion that seats were first placed in churches because of the congregation's need to sit for long periods. However, parish clergy had been preaching from at least the thirteenth century: the sermon was not a Protestant innovation but it received greater emphasis.[69] Seats were clearly part of many pre-Reformation churches in Devon and it is likely more would be revealed had a greater number of

Dolton.

Landcross.

records survived. In Devon church houses were erected at such places as Tawstock in 1477, Alphington in 1499, Abbotskerswell by 1524, Hockworthy in 1525 and Winkleigh in 1534.[70] This was the period of Devon's great church rebuilding and enlarging of the late fifteenth and early sixteenth century when parishes could afford to have a separate building for more riotous public celebrations. Also, like churches, benches and forms were in church houses.[71] It may be that the difference between the two buildings was that the seats in churches were more likely to be fixed in place although Sampford Courtenay's church house has early fixed furniture.[72]

There are two outstanding Elizabethan accounts for the building of seats. One is for Woodbury for the year 1572. In the churchwardens' account it was recorded:

'paid to Richard Yeost for timber to make new seats in the church 40s; paid to Thomas Adams for timber and for carriage of the same 6s 2d; paid to Andrew Hollwille for carriage of one load of timber from Salterton 2s; paid to Thomas Scorche for 6 boards & for carriage of the same from Otterton 3s 6d; paid to John Hoppin for carriage of timber from Salterton 6d; paid to Lawrence Elliate and one to help him to saw the same timber 18d; to the same Lawrence for 7 days 5s 10d; paid to 2 of Thomas Scorche's men for sawing of timber about the same work 2s 4d; for nails for the same work 13d; paid to Thomas Scorche for making of the new seats 40s; paid to one to rip up the 3 greater of tiles where now the new seats stand 11d; to James Crofte for carrying away the earth of the same places 9d; to Michell of Exmouth for laying of the tiles in the church 4s 7d.'[73]

Seven years later Crediton erected new seats. Their account noted:

'paid for timber to make the new pews in the choir as followeth, first paid unto Thomas Moxsey for 11 planks 8 pegs and 15 half inch boards 22s; also paid unto George Trobridge gent 13s 4d and to the school master 5s for timber and planks 18s 4d; also paid more unto Hugh Mortimer for 9 planks 9s; also paid unto Hill the joiner for 20 of muntins 10s; for 24 half inch

boards 10s and for other timber 10s 30s; also paid more unto Hill and Philip Bokenham for the carriage of the same timber 9s and for the seeking of it for 3 days' work 2s 6d 11s 6d; also paid more unto Hill and his man for one day's ripping work of the old seats 20d; also paid Venycome and Trewman and Hornell and Trewman [sic] for 12 days' sawing work after 28d the day 20s year is [20s]; also paid Hill more for 128 days' work about the new seats and other work in the church after 10d the day for his wages and table £5 6s 6d.[74]

The account shows that Richard Hill was employed for more than four months. Earlier that year he had spent two days 'ripping and fitting' the old seats in the choir. He was one of many working on the seats and the account also noted:

'paid unto Honywill & Southcott for 600 of hatch nails occupied about the seats and the bells 5s. Also paid more for 300 of board nails at 18d the hundred 4s 6d. Also paid for 150 of great brads 2s 8d for 200 of small brads 20d and 200 of other small nails 9d occupied about the seats 5s 1d. Also paid for the making of 16 pair of jimmies for the seats after the pair 8s, and for the mending one jimmies of the choir door 6d 8s 6d. Also paid for cramps, spanges, plates and great spokes occupied and made for the old seats and the new 21d'.[75]

Above: *Dartmouth St Saviour's church account with entries relating to new seats, 1555.*

These building accounts show the churchwardens were mainly concerned with recording costs. Additional information was recorded for two periods of installing earlier seats at Dartmouth St Saviours. The churchwardens noted for 1544:

'to Roger Gon for a transom 2d; to Hugh Tanner for 50 of boards, nails and 50 hatch nails for the pews at church 8½d; to Hugh Tanner for 5 sawn boards 20d; to Nicholas Smith for 12 transoms and the bringing from Totnes for the pews 2s 11d; to Roger Gon for 5½ days' work 22d; to John Jakman junior for 12 days' work at 3½d a day upon

the same pews 3s 6d; to John Jakman the elder for 16 days'
work upon the same pews 5s 4d; for 33 days and a half
meat and drink for the said 2 Jakmans and Gon 8s 3d;
for 3 pair of jimmies for the said pews at 8d a pair 2s; to
Nicholas Smith for 100 foot of boards and for bringing of
them from Totnes 2s 10d'.[76]

Dartmouth Corporation was the patron of St
Saviour's Church and the mayor ordered reseating ten
years later. Seat rentals had been recorded for a century
but that year, 1555, nearly 50 entries regarding seats were
entered. The scribe also recorded:

'When the new seats were made in the church at Mr
Mayor's commandment John Tanner the elder, Mistress
Adams the elder, Sibyl Hawkins, Pentecost Walker,
Katherine Hacker and Richard Wycks, Wilmot Winchester,
Amis Rich, Nicholl Soper, Martin Jackeman, Isabel Tryggs,
Emlyn Arthur and many more honest wives were removed
into higher seats and others lost their seats whereas they
afore did sit and all this was for the advantage of the town
and of the church'.

No less than £47 7s 8d had been raised. The
accounts detail further extensive work that year
including making seats from beech and fir wood.[77]
The extent of the Dartmouth records, and that
the Corporation was the patron of the church, provide
more fulsome details than those possible for any other
Devon church. The accounts not only record individuals
but technical and sometimes archaic terms such as a brad
(a headless nail), hatch nails (a rectangular rose-headed
nail), jimmy (a hinge), muntin (an upright bar), studdle
(a timber support) and transom (another form of timber
support). The references to seats begin with the earliest
churchwardens' accounts and subsequent records show
substantial seat rebuilding and renovation through the
fifteenth and sixteenth centuries. If other places
in Devon were similar to Dartmouth then church
seats were commonplace by the second half of the
fifteenth century.

Pews
1600 to the early 1800s

By the early 1600s the popularity of benches was diminishing in Devon's churches and high pews had begun to take their place. The earliest dated pew is at Hittisleigh where the squire had his erected at the head of the north aisle.

Molland's high pews and the Bluett family seat at Holcombe Rogus.

On it was carved *'this was built at the cost of Thomas Furse of East Church gentleman 1619'*. A wealthy member of the parish would have most likely led a new fashion. There are other impressive pews that were the preserve of high status families such as the Pine-Coffins at Alwington. An individual enclosed seat for the Bourchiers, the earls of Bath, is at Tawstock. Most others have not survived including one for the Walronds at Seaton. This had an oak canopy with carvings of foliage and eleven coats of arms.[78]

These seats neatly identified the superiority of their social positions. The great pew at Holcombe Rogus of the Bluett family is one of the grandest in Devon. It has stylistic similarities with carving in the church at Curry Mallet in Somerset. Both feature Biblical roundels including temptation in the Garden of Eden and the subsequent expulsion of Adam and Eve. The construction and figures are strikingly similar and the latter medallion appears to be the work of the same craftsmen or at least they were inspired by the same illustration. The carvings are thought to be Jacobean. In the church at Holcombe Rogus is also the memorial to Sir John

Above: *A Holcombe Rogus medallion.*
Below: *Similar carving at Curry Mallet, Somerset.*

Bluett who is credited with having had the pew built. Sir John's wife Elizabeth was born in Orchard Portman which is only five miles from Curry Mallet. A pew of comparable size and date has survived, in part, in the Cornish church of St Martin's near Looe.

The Fulford family pew at Dunsford is one of many still surviving across Devon and it also demonstrates how much room the great families had in a church. In contrast only a portion of the Arscott family pew survives at Tetcott but the carving indicates a grand seat. Parts of what might have been a family pew is at Peter Tavy. A door has been cut into it but whether these two long sections of Renaissance panels are the remnants of a pew is speculative.

Sir John Bluett.

The first half of the seventeenth century was transitional in seating in moving from benches to high pews but Devon has few examples of these seats.[79] The church at Plympton St Mary has retained a set of heraldic panels, with one dated 1637, which were fixed to the seating which belonged to the Stroude family. The seats themselves were destroyed only a few years ago. The bordering parish of Landulph in Cornwall has kept what would have been similar panels but these clearly show these were tall boxed-in pews. The carving is elaborate, Renaissance in style and features heraldic imagery. In this instance each of the panels, which are dated 1631, were carved in a similar manner to a bench end and in great contrast to the later box pews. There are other Cornish churches with similar examples.[80]

Detail of the seat at Plympton St Mary, 1637.

Monkleigh has several carved seventeenth-century high doors and High Bickington also has an example of a transitional seat: it has a pew with a door panel carved with a coat of arms and the initials 'R P'. Somerset has more surviving examples of these early pews in its churches notably at Mudford and Croscombe.[81]

High pews became plainer with less carving. They could also be simple in the early seventeenth century.

In 1626 Okehampton Corporation erected seats for the councillors in the parish church as well as new seats in St James Chapel within the town. A bench of three seats, with plain ends, survives.[82] Hatherleigh has a more elaborate example of later carving.

It may be that bench ends were still being erected in Devon but the lack of any with dates makes this difficult to verify. In comparison, Somerset has a number of early seventeenth seats, mostly high pews with carving on the ends, but there is also a small collection of bench ends with dates at Stringston. Lettering was crudely carved into many of these plain ends but one also has the date 1602 and another, at Cheddon Fitzpaine, is as late as 1660.

It is likely that by 1600 nearly every Devon church was filled with benches and any new building was to replace or upgrade existing seats. The Exeter Diocese's church court's records have many cases involving individuals seeking to upgrade their benches in the seventeenth and eighteenth centuries. For instance, by 1738 some of the ancient seats at Rattery were considered too small for comfort. One parishioner argued for permission to pull down his family's benches that were only two feet and five inches high. He wanted to replace them with new seats which were four feet and six inches in height.[83] Comfort has been one of the enduring criteria for seats but the move towards high pews was probably led as much, if not more so, by the desire to enhance privacy, increase warmth in winter and emphasise the occupier's higher social position.

Some parishes, perhaps led by financially prudent churchwardens, did not eject their benches but merely adapted them to fit the new fashion by adding doors. They had placed doors on benches from at least 1581 in Devon.[84] These helped to demarcate ownership as well as decrease draughts. Honeychurch has a door which might

Honeychurch's early door.

be an early example. The doors, and their locks, were not always popular: at Clyst Hydon a door was erected but it was removed by other parishioners and when it reappeared twenty years later there was 'perfect uproar'.[85] Doors became one of the hallmarks of a pew. A number of churches also retained their benches by enclosing them within pew frames. Torbryan has its medieval benches still encased in later wood. In 1945 the rector wanted to take out the high pews but he was told by the Diocesan Advisory Committee 'the whole effect is pleasing, characteristic and a valuable example of the continuity of history'.[86]

Entire churches were re-seated with pews such as Otterton in 1754, Blackawton in 1762 and Bradninch in

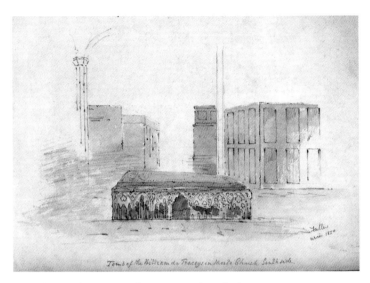

Mortehoe in the nineteenth century with its high pews.

1770.[87] Individual' applications for conversions concerned such places as Sidbury in 1713 where two seats were to 'be enclosed and erected into a pew',[88] Pinhoe's old benches were said to be 'sealed up' in 1709,[89] and Monkleigh had a seat which was 'pewed in and enclosed' in 1691.[90] Some of the church court records describe the physical form of these new seats. For example, in 1672 one parish had a 'round seat',[91] in 1693 Marldon's churchwardens sought to take down two ancient pews and erect in their place a 'square pew'[92] and at Woodland in 1701 the pew was described as having the form of a carpenter's square. The latter was in size 7 feet by 4½ feet.[93]

The size could be controversial. In 1699 a Cornwood parishioner complained that a seat was 5 or 6 inches higher than the one it replaced and blocked his view.[94] Clayhidon had the same complaint in raising the height of a seat by 20 inches and the minister and churchwardens, it was said, were not able to monitor the behaviour of the congregation.[95] A new seat was built at Cadbury in 1744, which was five feet and one inch in length, two to three feet in width and four feet and six inches in height. It was higher than the adjoining seats, by eleven and a half inches, but this was not the only problem: it blocked the aisle.[96] The same problem at Buckland Monachorum was solved in 1662 by cutting six inches off the form in the aisle. William Drake's new pew was then able to fit into the south aisle.[97]

There are few churches in Devon left with complete sets of box pews. Exceptional examples of full

Mortehoe's mix of ancient bench ends and high pews in the 1800s.

or part series can be seen at Cornworthy, Cruwys Morchard, Exeter St Martin, Gittisham, Halwell, Molland, Offwell, Poughill, Torbryan, West Ogwell and Whimple. Remains of high pews can be found in a great number of local churches. These, such as at Broadhempston, were reused as panelling and at Monkleigh, among many others, parts of the high pews were later used to make new benches.

When parishes replaced their seats in their entirety, such as at Cruwys Morchard after its fire, there was no choice other than pews. Tiered seating, useful for musicians, was in Devon by at least the 1760s: Cadeleigh had them by 1766 and at Colebrooke it was three years earlier. These 'raising seats' were specified as rising ten inches with its tier.[98] Their equivalent at Bickleigh near Tiverton comprised raising the existing bench ends at the west end of the church. Another good example of rising seats can be found at Parracombe St Petrock.

Social demarcations continued if not increased. In 1807 there was reseating at Dolton and after the best seats were reserved for the better-off the

Buckland Monachorum's mix of seats, 1832.

remainder, on 'the right hand side of the gallery', were 'to be occupied by the husbandmen and artificiers and the left by the females'.[99] The church courts continued to be busy through the eighteenth century with cases of disputed ownership and permissions for new seats. In one controversy the mayor of Okehampton wrote to the bishop pleading the case of a 'particular friend' who was in contention with a non-conformist who insisted on keeping his seat. The mayor added at the bottom of his letter that his friend intended to vote for the bishop's candidate in the forthcoming election.[100]

By the end of the eighteenth century the box pew had found its detractors. Some occupants had abused their space by erecting curtains.[101] In 1775 one writer, in a discussion on Moretonhampstead Church, dismissed pews as 'sleeping boxes'[102] as did much later the new cleric at Ringmore near Plymouth who embellished the insult by calling them 'the worn and rugged sleeping boxes'.[103] The bulkiness of the pews had also distorted the space in some churches. Of the monuments at Lustleigh it was said they 'are unfortunately much chipped about the arms by the modern barbarism of coarse churchwardens, to make room for these distortions which encumber many country churches, misnamed pews.'[104]

The afore-mentioned cleric at Ringmore was typical of the Victorian who denounced the high pew. Reverend Hingeston-Randolph found 'the pews, of every conceivable size and shape and height and colour, rotten and ruinous, were breaking down, every now and then, in service time, under their hapless inhabitants'.[105] His remedy was simple. He wrote:

'that terrible array of high-backed-pews, which I had found to be simply unbearable, and a serious hindrance to my work: the people were buried in them so effectively that I could not see a single soul when, at Communion time, I turned to read Epistle, Gospel or Exhortation! So, one Saturday afternoon, the whole of the ghastly and disgraceful enclosures fell to a decent and uniform height under the saws of the village carpenter and myself, to the great amazement of the congregation the following morning. Some of them told me that they felt, at first, rather naked and chill in the region which had been so long encased but they soon found and appreciated the convenience and comfort of the change.'[106]

What made this destruction all the more interesting is that it coincided with the return to favour of the bench. After 200 years of neglect, benches were once more fashionable.

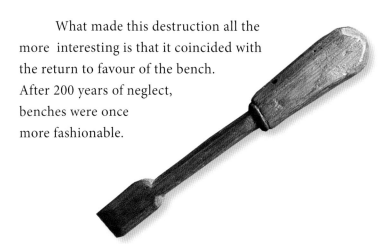

The nineteenth-century renaissance of the bench

The late medieval period and the years following the Reformation were the heyday of the creation of Devon's benches but during the following two centuries they not only became unfashionable but thousands were destroyed. The nineteenth-century saw a reawakening of interest.

The ancient benches became appreciated for their craftsmanship and thousands of new ones were carved. The first decades of the 1800s began the Renaissance of the bench end.

In 1822 'R.C.R.' wrote to the editor of the *Gentleman's Magazine* in the hopes of rescuing, through his publication, the bench ends in the church of Down St Mary from the

Details from restored bench ends at George Nympton showing the old and Victorian carving.

'*rude hands of violence and time*'. Restoration of the building had been agreed and the writer sent images of some of the bench ends.[107] They remain in the church although it cannot be determined if his letter had any impact. Six years later, in 1828, the Reverend John Pike Jones of North Bovey was another of the first Devonians to raise his voice in reappraising local bench ends. 'Bovey' Jones, as he was known, wrote in *The Ecclesiastical Antiquities of Devon and Cornwall*:

'*the modern pews of different heights and sizes are a great deformity; it was never intended in places of public worship that a certain class of persons should be shut in with high partitions, to talk or to sleep unobserved by the rest of the congregation. The old open seats are*

One of Ashwater's high pews cut down for use as a seat and a Victorian bench end.

best fitted to display the beauties of the church as well as to accommodate the public'.[108]

His co-author, the Reverend George Oliver, the well-known Roman Catholic priest and historian of Exeter, made his thoughts clear when he expressed:

'those sheep pens were introduced gradually towards the end of Queen Elizabeth's reign when Puritanism began to acquire strength and became fashionable during the reign of her tasteless successor'.[109]

The two men shared similar views on church architecture. Oliver was to eclipse Jones in both research and publication while Jones was remembered after his death for being active in politics. He was described as 'a great radical'.[110] In their volume Reverend Jones praised, amongst others, the benches at Kenn but he damned pews.

'On entering the church I was agreeably surprised at seeing so many of the old and solid praying benches, some of which are beautifully carved. In every respect they are better calculated to inspire devotion and a sense of humility in the presence of that Supreme Being... than towering and overgrown pews. And who will say that their simple form does not harmonise better with the fabric than boxes of every shape and colour?'[111]

The success of these views can be seen in a comment by a churchwarden from Hatherleigh nearly a generation later. John Smale Short thought it was a 'sad disgrace' that seats were not sufficiently low and disapproved of seating which had a distinction between the rich in their high seats and the poor in their lower ones behind them. Short quoted Bishop Ives:

'Where in our churches is the place for the poor? Admit that here and there a poor person has a seat: where is it? Is he invited to sit with us <u>in a good place</u> or do we say to him **Stand thou there or sit here under my footstool?'** [112]

Benches had taken on a social significance with the Victorian appraisal of how social distinction in church seating was anti-Christian. It was partly because of this that the first issue of the transactions of the Exeter Diocesan Architectural Society, in 1843, noted the importance of open seats.[113] The society had been founded two years previously. It followed shortly after the establishment of the Cambridge Camden Society, and the Oxford Movement before it, which sought to return Church of England architecture to its medieval beginnings. One of these ways was to reintroduce benches.[114]

In its early years the Society published the first survey of Devon's seating as part of a larger report on all local churches. It made withering judgements on pews including of

A bench end at Kenn which was highly approved of by Bovey Jones.

Beer ('pews of the worst sort, without the possibility of kneeling'), of South Tawton ('twenty years since, open benches prevailed: now not one is to be found'), of Hittisleigh ('all the open benches removed eight years since, are replaced by low deal except the Bradley pew, and one high one placed *a week since*') and of Kingsteignton 'a fine drawing room pew, with chairs, carpet etc., belonging to Mr Watts'. As well as damning the pews it also commended the benches. For instance, it commented on Hartland's chancel with one word – **'Pews!'** but of the nave:

'the whole of the benches west of the screen are open and good, in excellent preservation'.

The details on the survival of benches provide crucial evidence. The report noted churches which still have their bench ends such as Swimbridge ('no benches remain but parts of very good carving are cut up for support of the pews'), Tawstock ('the pens and monuments are frightful whilst a few good carved benches still remain'), Doddiscombsleigh ('good carved seats converted into pews'), Tedburn St Mary ('a few old seats'), Frithelstock ('good bench ends like Braunton'), Alwington ('some good bench ends remain in use'), Welcombe ('plain open oak benches. The seat ends have poppy heads'), West Woolfardisworthy ('many seat ends'), Satterleigh ('open seats with carved ends'), Torbryan ('the old seating remains in the nave, raised twelve inches and closed with oak doors') and Lewtrenchard ('in this church the carved seats remain, on north side there is a grotesque carving, the Angel of Judgement with sword and balance, leading a dragon, a female head with a youth beneath a cross, the implements of the crucifixion'). It also noted seats that have disappeared such as those at Manaton ('four old seats') and Pancrasweek ('good late bench ends').

The report's comment on Tavistock showed the change in thinking. It noted:

'this church is undergoing the entire process of new seating after the pattern of one end found amongst the old pews'.

Of Puddington it reported that *'every seat is open and of oak after old patterns'.*

The report also noted the importance of providing seats for all classes. Of South Molton it disapproved of the fittings:

'but here censure must give way to praise of the adoption of an unusual, but most desirable, appropriation of the seating – the poor being accommodated in the centre of the ground floor, the wealthier classes in and under the galleries'.[115]

Across Victorian Devon churches took out their pews and replaced them with benches. At Crediton Church's reopening the Dean of Exeter said to great applause:

'he was heartily glad when the vicar put the hammer and axe to the old pews and now they all had the gratification to know they were all got rid of.'[116]

At St Olaves in Exeter new oak seats were built partly with the remnants of old pews[117] while at Great Torrington oak seats were likewise fashioned from the galleries, which had been taken down.[118] Like those of Tavistock, Clyst St George resurrected the design of old seats.[119] In 1867 Tedburn St Mary asked the public for funds to change the seats. An advert noted 'large uneven high square pews which in many instances have been built upon fine old oak low seats and hide handsomely-carved bench ends'.[120] The church at Churston Ferrers incorporated old carving in the new seats[121] as did its counterpart at George Nympton where fragments were retained in order to build new benches around them.

When Ashton reopened in 1883 the congregation found that the pews, which had been built on top of the ancient benches, were gone. Like today, they would have seen the deep cuts made into the church's stone columns to accommodate the pews. At the reopening it was noted that the ancient benches had been mutilated but that these ends were repaired and adapted to the new seats.[122]

The vicar at Swimbridge recounted the restoration of the church in 1881 following the box pews having been erected in 1782 and 1794. He explained *'the building was also blocked up with high old-fashioned deal pews, the old carved seats having been removed years ago to make way for the wretched horse box pews of the Georgian era. These have been supplanted with oak seats and some fragments of the old ones (which were made to do duty as props to the wretched deal seats which formerly disfigured the church) have been carefully preserved and worked with the new seating which has been carved to correspond with them. All the carving except the chancel stalls has been done by Charles Pickard of Barnstaple who has faithfully coped the old examples and has given the utmost satisfaction'.*[123]

Another church in North Devon also arranged for its seats to be restored: Mortehoe employed a local man, Mathew Isaacs of Barnstaple, to repair and replace the bench ends. By 1908 it was remembered only that there were 48 ancient benches which were 'restored and partly renewed when the church was restored in 1859'.[124] Careful

The carvings of what might be the head of John the Baptist at Mortehoe and Braunton.

examination shows that a portion of the seats are ancient. The remainder are copies of what had been in the church. The motifs were recorded in 1832 and the list tallies with many which can be seen today except for a series of initials, which have disappeared. Others have taken their place. One of the bench ends, of a hand holding a man's head, appears to copy another at Braunton but whether Isaacs himself copied an ancient one at Mortehoe or took the design from Braunton cannot be determined. The skill of the Victorian craftsmen, along with modern treatment of the wood, can all but obscure distinguishing the old from the new.

It may have been because of this renewed appreciation of benches that James Davidson came across an extraordinary sight in the church of Littleham near Bideford. He visited in 1848 and wrote of a screen he saw which separated the vestry from the nave. It was 'ornamented with panels worked in cement and painted to imitate old oak from which they can scarcely be distinguished. They were formed in moulds taken from the ends of the old oak benches in the church'.[125] The church was subsequently renovated and the screen then presumably destroyed.

Nineteenth-century news stories triumphed the restoration of churches and the renovation or reintroduction of benches. In 1854 the elaborate carving at Feniton by John Mason of Exeter was praised and two years later another Exeter man, William Rex, made new seats at Shillingford.[126] New seats were sometimes carved with the names of the workmen. The new roundels to the Bluett family pew at Holcombe Rogus have the name R. Frost carved along with the date 1880 and under the early-twentieth century benches at East Budleigh are three carpenters' names.[127]

No doubt many dozens of different individuals carved Victorian Devon's new benches but three names are particularly distinguished. Hems, Read and Pinwill should be remembered for outstanding contributions to local carving in the second half of the nineteenth century. What makes their legacy all the more interesting is that

The illustrious Harry Hems.

dozens of other men and women were also carving wood in Devon.

Harry Hems is the greatest name in the history of Devon woodcarving. The tale of his arrival in Exeter became legendary, in part because of Hems' extraordinary other gift, for self-publicity. No other Devonian had ever generated as many reports in newspapers across the world. Hems was a gifted carver but his real talent lay in organising a carving business at Exeter which became world-wide.

Harry Hems was born in London in 1842 and came to Exeter twenty-four years after having been trained at the Sheffield School of Art. Hems later described his master as being 'a miserable little fellow who was a singularly talented carver of wood'. As important as this training was, Hems also benefitted from working as a journeyman carver not only throughout Great Britain but also on the continent. For three years, from 1863 to 1866, Hems received an education on the road and was able to observe a wealth of ancient carving. Later he became an experienced traveller with trips to Africa and the United States.

Hems arrived in Exeter in 1866 having been asked to help carve the stonework for the new city museum. Upon disembarking from the train he found a horseshoe. This he kept as a talisman and eventually placed it above the door of his Exeter workshop which he named the Lucky Horseshoe Studio. The work appears to have been too great for him alone and he brought down from London some former colleagues, men he described as 'hobbledehoys' and elsewhere as lusty young fellows. Hems' business, the Ecclesiastical Art Works, eventually employed more than 80 men and he was unrivalled for self-publicity. He let it be known that by the end of his first decade in business he had placed work in over a thousand churches. Hems acquired an international reputation; through his work being featured in international exhibitions he was commissioned to supply carvings for buildings across the globe. In one instance, in 1882, he needed a model for Lucifer and advertised for 'an old man, must be <u>very</u> ugly, and have a large mouth. None others need apply'. Hems' work was continued by his sons but after his death in 1916 the firm, Hems & Sons, dwindled in importance and influence.

Hems proudly wrote that he did not employ any foreign men and while there were several widely-publicised cases of physical abuse by Hems against his staff there were also many reports of the loyalty of his men to him and also of him to them.

Harry Hems arrived in Devon just as local churches were being renovated and rebuilt. There was a strong demand for carved wood and stone. Benches became of particular interest to Hems who sent hundreds of reports and photographs of his work to national newspapers. Typical is an enthusiastic account of the restoration of Northlew in 1885. One journalist reported 'it will be a matter of deep rejoicing to every lover of our local antiquities that the whole series of these medieval seats was placed in the skilful hands of Mr Harry Hems of Exeter, the well-known carver, and have now been returned to the sacred fane in which they had for nearly four hundred years done previous duty, restored into precisely so good a condition as they were the first day they left the maker's hands.'[128]

Hems' work at Stowford in 1874 shows the intensity of his endeavours. The task at this church was unlike

A Stowford bench end based on one at Ottery St Mary, see page 131.

anything Hems had previously undertaken. In effect, Hems created a Victorian museum of local bench ends. Sir Gilbert Scott, then working at Exeter Cathedral, was employed as the architect and the rector sent his clerk of works to travel through North Devon and Cornwall to take plaster casts of the 'best' bench ends. These were then sent to Hems who had the benches carved in Exeter. The rector later wrote that the 'the chief part of which was done by two very clever London men – Dyer and Moultrie'.[129] Ottery St Mary, Abbotsham, Landcross and Weare Giffard are among the churches that were visited for their bench ends. Examples of their bench ends can be found in the church along with others which do not appear to have survived in churches in either Devon or Cornwall.

More typical may be the work that his firm undertook at Noss Mayo in 1883. *The British Architect* praised the carving for 'its vigour and character'.[130] Hems had in his care the carving of nearly one hundred bench ends and these show medieval Devon design as well as Victorian creativity in different motifs. *The Illustrated Carver and Builder* concluded that Hems 'is now unrivalled in reputation'.[131] The output of work from Harry Hems & Sons needs to be seen as having been completed in what was a very large operation and seldom having been the work of Hems himself. He was not bashful in talking about his success and encouraged others to also do so. It was commonly said that Hems had

considerable energy and talent but one observer noted that his secret lay in Hem's implicit belief in himself.[132]

In 1892 Herbert Read, a former employee of Hems, set up his own firm. The Saint Sidwell's Art Works was situated not only in Exeter but very near to the Hems' studio. The first year of the firm was not one of easy relations between the two men. The thirty-two year old Read announced his firm was open for business and a bitter exchange of words between the two men appeared in the press. Read had been Hems' manager and general foreman but Hems publicly stated that Read had no experience as either a sculptor or carver. Read was followed in the business by his son Herbert and then by his grandson Herbert (known as Dick). It is unlikely that Hems and Read were again on friendly terms.

Read's firm rose in prominence as Hems' diminished. Exeter lay at the heart of the diocese's church restorations but the two firms competed for work far beyond the county borders. Read had considerable success. The firm's work in bench ends is impressive. Read's carvings at Dunchideock demonstrate careful craftsmanship. New benches copy the existing ones seamlessly so that it is difficult to tell one from the other.

Left: Noss Mayo.
Above: Herbert Read's work at Lydford.

63

The benches at Lydford show another side to the Read firm. In 1923 it produced 79 benches of religious figures comprising 'prophets, martyrs, saints and confessors' to illustrate the histories of the Jewish and Christian churches. Amongst these figures are Mungo Park, David Livingstone and General Charles Gordon.[133] There is a similar style to each of them but differing foliage and animals within the borders.

The third force in Devon's church carvings was unusual partly in being based in Plymouth but more so for being led by women. Violet Pinwill was one of the most dynamic forces in church furnishings in Devon. She

The Pinwill daughters with three male colleagues.

has been credited with work in scores of churches across the West Country but, like her competitors Hems and Read, her reputation has overshadowed the contributions of others working alongside her.

In 1874 Reverend Edmund Pinwill moved from Lincoln to become rector of Ermington in south Devon. He and his wife had seven daughters ranging from Grace (born in 1869) to Ruth (born 1878). According to family tradition Reverend Pinwill gained the nickname 'the Pope' after he placed a cross on the altar. One result was that local people pelted the Pinwill daughters with rotten apples whilst the girls walked with their nurse. Pinwill raised sufficient funds to restore his church and John Sedding, a London architect, was employed to oversee the work. He brought with him his nephew Edmund Harold Sedding and according to the Census of 1891 he was then a visitor at the vicarage. The church restoration was completed in 1889 but while it was being done Mrs Pinwill engaged the workmen to teach her daughters carving lessons during the evenings in the harness room above the stables. Two years later the census noted that three of the Pinwill sisters, Mary Rashleigh, Annie Ethel and Violet Alice, were professional carvers of wood.

Amongst their first works were the pulpits at Stoke Fleming and Ermington. The pulpit at Stoke Fleming was completed in 1891 when Violet Pinwill was only seventeen years old and the sisters were given the commission by Edmund Sedding. He also designed the

The Pinwills' work at Highweek.

pulpit.[134] Ten years later the census recorded another visitor, Edmund Sedding, aged eight. His father Edmund was then living with his sister Florence in Cornwall.

The eldest sister, Mary Rashleigh Pinwill, then aged 22, appears to have been the initial leading force. She named the undertaking after herself but did not use her first name: it was called Rashleigh Pinwill & Company. In about 1900 the Pinwill sisters moved their operations to Plymouth but five years later their workshop was destroyed by fire. They continued the business and

65

employed a number of men as carvers. An early photograph of the sisters shows them with three men 'Smith, Flashman and Giles' who were identified as a modeller, joiner and carver. These were presumably the men who taught the girls how to carve.

Their work at Plympton St Mary is exceptional. Sedding had once more commissioned the sisters. There is richness to the carving and the natural history detail of the poppy heads is exacting. Exbourne is another fine example of their work. Here the women used traditional Devon bench end themes in Gothic tracery and foliage and heraldry but the carving is vigorous and imaginative. Sheepstor also shows the inventiveness that must have been expressive of the commissioner as well of the carver.

The Pinwill sisters contributed work to many Devon churches but unfortunately much of it in Plymouth was destroyed during the bombing of the early 1940s. Violet was the only sister to remain with the business and died in 1957.[135]

In addition to these three firms many other carvers worked independently on Devon benches in many other churches. Some are known in only one building. Two bench ends at Sherford were carved with 1898, 'Keynedon Manor' and the initials 'deh'. Iddesleigh has woodwork by two Victorian parishioners, Tom Simmons and Miss Arnold of Nethercott. The benches at Alwington were supplemented in the early twentieth century by the work of Reuben Arnold. His work is now known as 'the Alwington Bible'. At Monkleigh it was a local man, Lewis Ellis, carpenter and sexton, who renovated the benches in the 1870s.[136] Hems, Read and Pinwill dominated the erecting of Devon's later benches but it needs to be appreciated much work was by their employees and by a range of craftsmen working independently of them.

Above: Sheepstor.
Left: *Plymouth St Mary.*

Alwington.

An unusual carving at East Budleigh.

PART TWO

THE IMPORTANCE
OF THE RIGHT SEAT

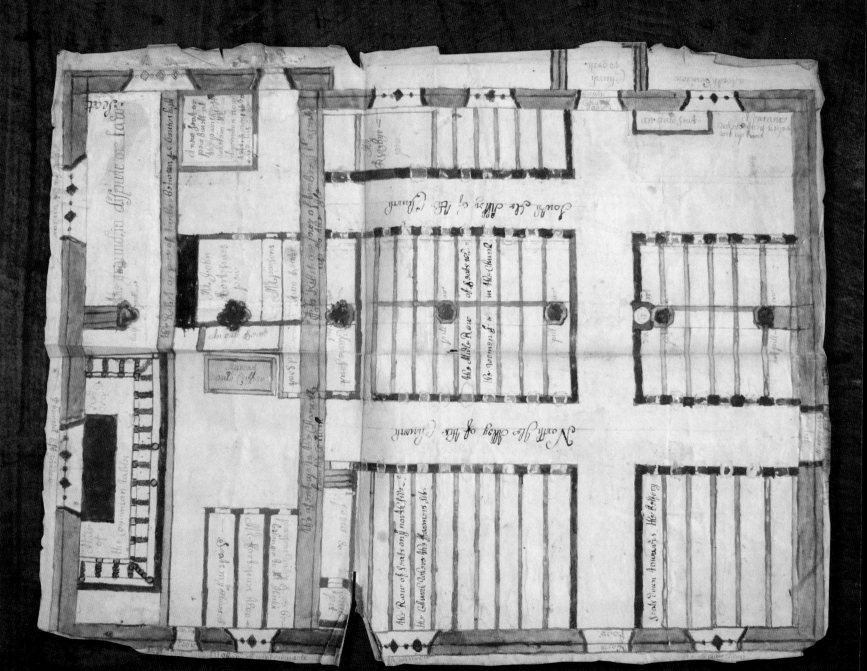

his own seat concerns Jonathan Sparke, a merchant of Plymouth. He agreed in 1646, during the Parliamentary siege of the town, that he would pay one hundred pounds towards building Plymouth's second church, Charles, on condition that he would have ownership of two to three seats in perpetuity. He was allowed to choose any place in the church once the mayor and magistrates had chosen theirs'.[147]

These systems were used in many country churches but it was not the practice in urban ones. In these places, where wealth was poorly defined by land holdings, another formula had to be used. At Tiverton each seat was rented to the highest bidder and that seat remained with each individual as long as he paid rent. A widow could continue in her husband's seat with the same stipulation.[148] Barnstaple also rented seats and this was also the practice at Ilfracombe, Dartmouth and Plympton St Erle. The latter parish appointed two 'seat-setters' each year and their account was kept separately from the parish rate.[149] Seat-holders at Barnstaple kept their places as long as they continued to live in the town.[150] Plymouth St Andrew's kept the same tradition

Buckerell's seats including those for Witch Farmhouse, 1773.

for several centuries: by 1637 all seats were rented for a lifetime's interest and the fee was dependent upon the 'relative situation and condition of the pew'.[151]

Social status rose with the proximity to the eastern end of the nave, or to be more precise, to the parson and his pulpit. It was because of this that a farmer at Wembury refused to sit at the west end of the nave; he complained 'workmen and labourers and servants will then be nearer the pulpit than himself'.[152]

The family that held the advowson, the right to appoint the vicar or rector, often had its own seats either at the head of the nave, within a family chapel or possibly in the chancel itself. They would naturally have been among the principal landholders if not the main one. Thus, the Raleigh bench at East Budleigh is located at the head of the nave.

There were also special seats for clerics and church officers. The vicar or rector was seated at the head of the church and this often included his family. In this respect his wife had a status which pre-empted those of the men. At Cruwys Morchard, and possibly elsewhere, the vicar's wife sat alongside the screen and directly across from the pulpit.[153] Churchwardens and other church officers were also given particular seats.

The cleric's seat had a function other than ease to the pulpit and communion table. It was here that other ceremonies took place such as in 1622 when John Rugg and Thomasine Dodd of Littleham at Exmouth stood to perform penance for their adultery. They were humiliated in public by being forced to stand clad in white sheets, without any shoes and had to bare their legs.[154] This position was important because of the prominence of the vicar's seat which was in full view of the congregation.

Manor houses, bartons and farms became associated with particular seats but there were further divisions according to gender. In some parishes the men sat at the head of the nave and wives sat behind them, sometimes directly, but in other parishes, such as Atherington,[155] the wife's seat was often at a distance. This may have been commonly practised throughout Devon but customs varied. At Stoke Damerel some men and women sat together in 1696.[156] Behind these rows of those that paid the parish rate, of

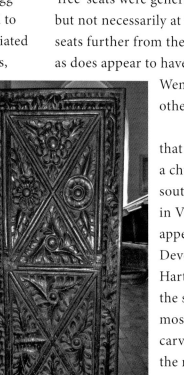

A bench end at North Tawton.

the financially-demarcated men, and then their wives who were similarly differentiated, sat those who were less wealthy. Each parish church appears to have retained, initially at first but less so by the early nineteenth century, some seats for those too impoverished to pay. These 'free' seats were generally at the western end of the nave but not necessarily at the furthest end. At Wembury the seats further from the minister were used by the poorest as does appear to have been the case at North Tawton. Wembury also had the poor in other places.

It has been accepted wisdom that women sat on the north side of a church while the men were in the south.[157] This was apparently the custom in Victorian Belstone[158] but it does not appear to have been widespread in Devon although it was the tradition at Hartland. Atherington's women sat on the south side in what is the row of the most ancient benches which have high carved finials.[159] At Black Torrington the men sat in seats at the front in the north, middle and south rows while the women sat behind them at the back of the church.[160] Elsewhere, such as West Ogwell, the men and women also sat in the same order.[161]

Sidbury with aisle seats in 1842.

Two types of aisle seats at Dartmouth St Saviour, 1842.

There were other demarcations. At Cornwood a form, the aforementioned backless plank of wood with four legs, was provided outside the bench where the chief landholder sat. The form was described as being 'on four legs not fastened to any seat'. It was in the aisle to be used by his servant boys and male apprentices from at least 1637 according to one witness.[162] Presumably it was important for the master to watch over his charges while also demonstrating his, and their, social status. In 1715 it was explained in North Petherwin that a bench was fixed to a seat to provide accommodation for servants. North Tawton also had benches in the aisles and these were not allocated to any particular individual; presumably the poor were too insignificant to merit noting by name. In Honiton the poor sat on a 'trap', the board fixed against the end of those seats along the aisles.[163] Engravings show these were at such churches as Sidbury and Dartmouth St Saviour's. Clovelly retains three of these early seats. Holy Trinity Church in Ilfracombe has kept its aisle seats: the church was reseated in the 1860s and the traps were fixed to the pine benches.

One of Clovelly's aisle seats.

Ilfracombe Holy Trinity retains its Victorian aisle seats.

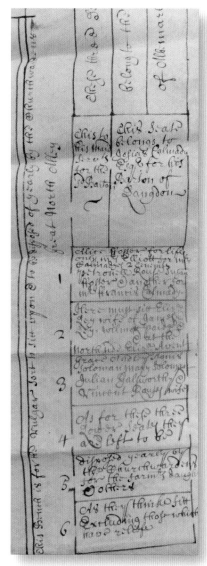

A detail from Wembury's plan showing the bench for the 'vulgar'.

By 1682 there was a bench placed along the north wall of Wembury's church 'for the vulgar sort to sit upon & to be disposed of yearly by the churchwardens'. It was here that sat the 'servant maids and the daughters of such as are no payers'. In contrast farmers' daughters were in the women's row of benches because they had fathers who contributed to the parish rates but sat in the last row because they were unmarried. Their brothers sat along the eastern wall of the south aisle and were with other young men. Between them and the congregation lay an enormous monument to the memory of Lady Narborough, a daughter of the resident gentry family, the Calmadys of Langdon Court. Around it sat the servants of another great landholder. The Calmady servants themselves had sat in a similar position from, it was later claimed, the late 1500s through to the end of the eighteenth century.[164] Aisle seats were probably used throughout Devon for those of low status. There was a form at Sidbury church in 1713 and most likely in every part of Devon.[165]

Age also separated the parishioners. In 1786 the chancel at Wembury was occupied by servants and it was claimed as a tradition for the previous 200 years[166] but in other places it was where children and teenagers sat. As with Widecombe-in-the-Moor in 1638, in Cornwood in 1699 and in Pinhoe ten years later the boys sat in seats provided around the communion table.[167] This was not always successful. In 1711 it was said of Ashprington that the 'younger sort' behaved indecently in the chancel in that they threw their hats upon the communion table.[168] There was a different seating custom at Ipplepen where in 1674 it was recorded that the parish clerk shared his seat with boys.[169] At Exmouth there were also seats provided around the south and north sides of the communion table in the chancel but the occupants were not specified on the plan.[170] Such seats still remain at St Martin's Church in Exeter.

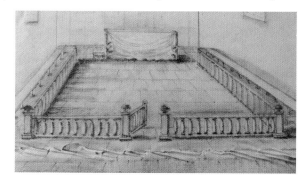

Pinhoe's eighteenth-century seats around the communion table.

Disability also was a factor. Some parishioners used it to obtain better seats. At Whitestone in 1699 one woman claimed she 'could not hear many words that were delivered by the minister in the pulpit' and needed to move to the front. A Woodland woman also argued that she wanted a seat nearer the vicar because she was 'somewhat hard of hearing'.[171] A Seaton man made the same claim in 1617.[172] The question of a Harberton's man's lack of sight was raised as a consideration in about 1619. Thomas Newton used three arguments for why he should have a particular seat. He declared that he was of better 'quality, parentage and lineage' than another man, Nicholas Tippett, but also that he paid an equal amount in taxes and his third point was that he was blind in both eyes and could not walk without being led. He added a cautionary warning perhaps in a plea for compassion: he was as blind 'as Nicholas Tippet in time may be'.[173]

There was a temporary demarcation which related to gender and specifically to child-bearing. The Church of England directed that women who had just given birth should sit in a particular seat.[174] Therefore, in 1666 Colebrooke women had a seat in order to 'sit and kneel in to return their thanks after child bearing'. There was a dispute over the ownership of it between the parish and a private individual: a Mr Prye was cited for destroying it.[175] At about the same time there was discussion in Milton Abbot on where to relocate its churching seat from its position near the reading desk.[176] Records also show a churching pew at Ashwater in 1762.[177] Hatherleigh allocated a place which would have had high status: the seat next to the pulpit was 'for women to sit in at their purification'.[178] Iddesleigh had one in the late 1600s[179] and Yarcombe had plans to build one in 1803.[180] These parish records show that particular seats were designated and the warden's accounts for Crediton illustrate how every year through the sixteenth century money was given for the women's 'purification'.[181] The custom, although unpopular with some Puritans,[182] continued through to the 1960s although it has not been determined if ancient churching pews were then used anywhere in Devon. Village tradition in Braunton is that their churching pew is the seat directly behind the font.[183] That bench end had its carving shaven off at some unknown point. Whether the carving represented women is a point of speculation.

Braunton's damaged Churching seat.

To the same article ... deposeth et dicit ... warded for the tyme beyng of [Isleham] ... the same part ... the ... expressed ... might be ... and ... by ... warden ... This [shee] ... [hee] hath ... the same ... dwelt in [Isleham] aforesaid et dicit ...

To the next article ... deposeth et dicit That about fourteene ... at the remembrance the [late] [Roger] [Everett] ... Will ... [Harris] beyng then wardens of [Isleham] ... did [plant] the ... [Marie] [Harris] in the [close] now in controversie, wch is the ... her [mother] ... her [life tyme] did [use] to [sitt] ... and reddit [causam] [scientie] ... [semper] shee hath ... the [house] in the parishe [church] of [Isleham] aforesaid ... the said [Marie] [Harris] [planted] as aforesaid et dicit ... et [aliter] nescit deposere et dicit

To the fourth article [next before] depos' et dicit That the [late] [Marie] ... did after her [planting] as aforesaid quietly & [peaceably] [enioye] the said ... aforesaid [till] her [going] to London (but how longe it was ...) And [saith] that the [close] ... the said [Marie] [Harris] was [planted] ... aforesaid ... the same [place] wch is now in controversie & [therein] ... [did] [use] to [sitt] et [ita] depos' ex [certa] [scientia] ... et dicit Et [aliter] nescit deposere et dicit

To the [seaventh] article nescit deposere et dicit

And [to the] last dicit [quod] deposita [vera] ...

Disputes

In 1631 churchwardens in a Cornish part of the Exeter diocese felt able to write with confidence that the seats were allocated 'according to the ancient custom'.[184] They would have been all too aware of the potential for disagreements caused by seating plans whether there was an ancient custom or not.

Great insights into how Devonians regarded church seating can be found amongst the papers of the diocesan church court. This archive was housed in the south tower of Exeter Cathedral on the night of 3 May 1942 when the Luftwaffe bombed the city. A high explosive resulted in the destruction of many of the court's papers and the blast reorganised those that survived. Whilst many of the original court cases can only be partly understood because of this destruction, they nevertheless are important for the revelations that they provide.

A damaged church court deposition regarding Barnstaple and the aftermath of the bombing of Exeter Cathedral, May 1942.

One such case concerned a seat in the church of Butterleigh. In the spring of 1628 two sisters, Anne and Mary Babbacombe, were prosecuted for troubling fellow parishioner Anne Chattie: they jostled her in her seat and when reproved by the churchwarden they spoke irreverently and mocked him by 'making mouths'. Their father even pulled her out of the seat into the aisle. It transpired that the churchwarden who appointed Anne Chattie to that seat was her own father.[185] Many cases were concerned with disputes over the entitlement to seats. Two women of Yarnscombe near Barnstaple argued in 1638 over one particular seat. Katherine Hawkeridge, the wife of a carpenter, disputed the seat with Margaret Bellew who was married to a gentleman. Women who lived in a property called Westward, according to a great number of villagers, had sat in that church seat for more than fifty years. Richarda Boyles and Mellony Dillon testified that they heard the two women argue on a Sunday in April 1637.

Hawkeridge was in the disputed seat when she was approached by Bellew who said *'Sit further in Katherine'* who responded *'I will not'*. This was repeated and Bellew added *'I shall have my place, shall I not?'* Hawkeridge replied *'Why dost not thou see how other women do go to the other end of the seat, and so do thou.'* As Bellew kneeled down by the end of the seat Hawkeridge grabbed her tut and matt and threw them into the aisle. The second woman remembered slightly different details about the conversation. She thought Bellew said *'Shall not I come into my seat, Goodwife Hawkeridge?'* to which was replied *'Canst not thou go about as other women do?'*[186] What may seem a trivial matter was obviously of great importance to these women as were the disputes between many others across the diocese.

A seating plan for Hartland made in 1613 shows how the parishioners were all placed in order. It was made as a result of a dispute but nevertheless another argument arose shortly afterwards. Margaret Secombe contended that she was entitled to sit with Agnes Blackedown and Alice Prust in the fourth seat on the north side because her husband was the occupier of the farms of Gawlish and Titchberry.[187] The reseating had been preceded by a relocation only a few years before. Some parishioners had been allocated new places in 1598 and this was not an uncommon practice. A plan of Northam made in 1650 shows the great number of names crossed out and new ones added to each seat.[188] In some places there was clearly a frequent change in occupation while in others there was considerable continuity.

The number of disputes show that seating was an important issue. In the late 1600s North Tawton's churchwardens wrote that they needed to agree the ordering of their seats 'for the settling of love and peace' as well as 'for the avoiding of all differences

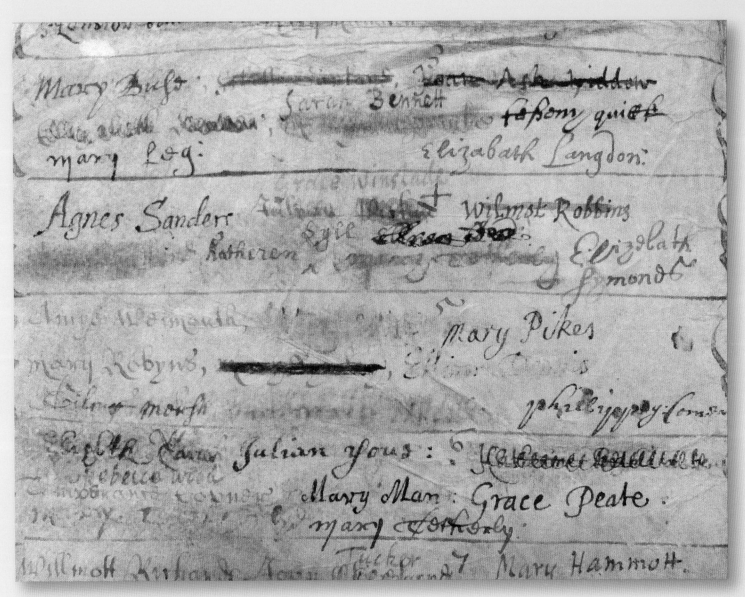

Detail of Northam's seating plan showing changes.

A deposition regarding a dispute over seating at Hartland.

that would otherwise arise'.[189] In the late 1600s there were years of 'divers disorder and dissensions' in the parish of High Bray over the seating plan.[190] Likewise, the prevention of disorder was given as the reason for new seating plans for Okehampton in 1663 and in parishes across Devon such as Mamhead from which a petition in 1619 to the bishop asked for a new plan to avoid 'contention and quarrelling'.[191]

Disputes could be heated and fierce. In 1774 two Chulmleigh women, while in a pew, quarrelled over who was entitled to sit in it. The seat was situated next to the pulpit and thus had high status. One woman went so far as to sit on the other's lap and allegedly said to her *'Bold, pert, impudent, audacious little thing, how can you be so bold to sit above me that am a married woman? Tis likely your impudence to keep and detain my goods, the whole town tells how impudent you are'.*[192] A similar row broke out in Honiton in 1765. Local woman Betty Earle tried to sit with other women in a long bench but was refused admission. It was alleged that one of them called her a wasting impudent slut. Earle was told to go to the aisle *'a place most fit for her'.* This she was loathe to do as it was where the poorest sat.[193]

Detail of a bench end at Ottery St Mary.

Disputes continued into the nineteenth century. One particularly acrimonious argument took place in 1842 when the vicar of Ottery St Mary contested with the governors of the church over ownership of a seat which had been occupied by the previous three vicars.

On the 2nd of January Reverend Sidney Cornish entered the pew on the day of his first service but two assistant governors removed him. Cornish subsequently took possession of the pew but found, on one Sunday in September, that other parishioners were seated there. They refused to leave and Cornish ordered the constable to eject them. Eventually all other claims to the seat ceased and Reverend Cornish was able to sit in the pew undisturbed.[194] The disputes reveal attitudes not just to a sense of entitlement but to the wider issues of social place and position. It may seem unlikely today that any one individual, let alone many hundreds, would initiate legal proceedings over a seat but there were even such disputes over where parishioners hung their hats. One argument at Cornwood took eight years to pass through the courts and had four appeals. The case was finally decided before three judges, two bishops and two peers of the realm. It was, wrote a later commentator, *'a pretty heavy hammer for so small a nut'.*[195]

Landcross figures.

PART THREE

THE BENCHES

The forms

The feature of the Devon bench which has most attracted the historian's attention is the carved end. It is seen to its best advantage whilst sitting across in a nearby bench: the gaze is then directly upon it and not distorting the perspective from above.

Left: High Bickington
Below: Weare Giffard.

Devon's benches are nearly always rectangular and the majority have flat tops. Weare Giffard and High Bickington are unusual in having notched tops.

Devon, in contrast to East Anglia and with neighbouring Somerset, does not have many surviving 'poppy heads', taken from the Latin *puppis*, a finial on the stern of a boat. Only a handful of parishes have them. The greatest number are at Atherington which has a dozen ends with great rising finials. The bench ends here are also asymmetrical which is rare for Devon although there are two similar ones at Cookbury and Crediton, possibly the remnants of a series of seats. The closest collection of asymmetrical bench ends is at Croscombe near Wells in Somerset. The church may have once been filled with them but there still remains several dozen. It is also rare for East Anglia although it can be found in Suffolk.[196]

Much more elaborate poppy heads can be seen on two benches at Ilsington. These have grand carving with additional figures representing the four evangelists which were added at a later date. Bridford also has carving added to former bench ends by 1843; these are known to have been reused from existing woodwork formerly in the church.[197]

Victorian drawing of Atherington's seats.

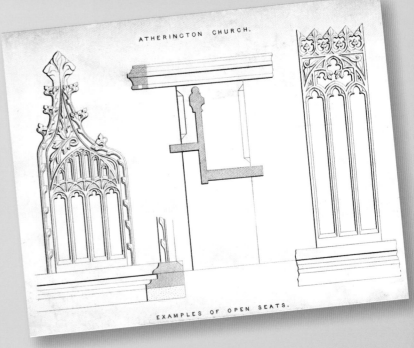

Atherington's unusual assymetrical seats.

Above and right: *Upton Hellion and Stockleigh Pomeroy.*

At Upton Hellions there can be seen a crouching single lion while Stockleigh Pomeroy has a salamander and a griffin on a reading desk. All three have had damage with those at the latter church more obviously defaced with intent. Those at Down St Mary were long ago sawn off. Each formed part of the first row of central benches near the chancel. The tail and hands of one creature only remain on one bench end while another creature on the corresponding end has a portion of its bottom half still on the bench. There is a similarly damaged bench end at nearby Lapford. Other Devon parish churches also had poppy heads. Sabine Baring Gould, the Victorian writer, noted of Welcombe 'there were interesting bench ends with very curious heads. At the 'restoration' a few of the ends were plastered against the screen, and their unique heads sawn away so as to make them fit the place into which they were thrust, but never designed to occupy.'[198] Today the four bench ends can still be seen reset within the screen and the tops have clearly been cut away. Two ancient loose finials have been retained although these are too large to have been originally used for these particular ends. There

Stockleigh Pomeroy.

89

is also a reading desk and seat which have repaired poppy heads. These are all grand seats and the church may have benefited from it being a medieval chapel of Hartland Abbey.[199] In Yarcombe there are two seats with carvings on the top of the reused bench ends. These have been greatly restored, replaced or possibly reinvented with good Victorian carving.

Three benches at Combe-in-Teignhead have fared better and these have five carvings of interest. Two front benches each have a figure with a carved stop. Behind and

Yarcombe.

The Combe-in-Teignhead lion.

below these on one bench is a crouching lion and on the other a bear in a cowl. A third bench has a dog chasing a fox who has taken a goose. These are little damaged.[200] The same cannot be said of those at Combe Martin which must have had very superior carving at one time. What appears to have been a dragon stands on one bench while on two others are the remains of what could have been birds. The fate of a fourth animal is worse: only

The Combe-in-Teignhead bear, and the dog chasing a fox.

The dog, fox and goose above the saints.

West Anstey.

High Bickington.

High Bickington.

Combe Martin.

the feet are left. There is an unidentified creature at West Anstey and a geometric poppy head at George Nympton.

As with Stockleigh Pomeroy, a griffin can be found at High Bickington but there is also a more unusual creature. This may once have been a lion but is now missing its head. What is peculiar is that it appears to have its front legs facing inwards. It might be St Luke's bull. These poppy heads and the others across Devon are all scanty remains and their importance lies in their being an indicator of what might have previously been a much richer history of carving.[201]

Other parts of the benches are also worth consideration. Beautiful workmanship can be found in the seat, back and rail as well

Bideford's tower screen possibly erected from a reading desk or family pew.

as in the carved fronts and backs of seat rows such as at Marwood. Carved ends can be found still serving their original purpose as well as being incorporated within the reredos at North Tawton or Alwington, as part of the tower screen at Bideford and being used to create pulpits in such varied churches as Buckland Brewer, Landcross and

93

reat profperitie giueth hee vnto his King ↄ ſheweth louing kindnets vnto dauid his anointed, ↄ vn

THE SCREEN BETWEEN THE CHANCEL & CHURCH THE CHURCH WAS NEW SEATED THE GALLERY REBUILT & ENLARGED IN THE YEAR 1550 REV·

Stockleigh Pomeroy. Parts of screens have been reused in similar schemes and it can be difficult to determine the original function of the carved panels. Thin panels generally appear to have first been carved for rood or gallery screens whereas the bench end itself was, in Devon, a considerably thicker piece of wood. There was also a Victorian practice of retaining the carved end and incorporating it within new seats. Many examples of this can be found throughout Devon and sometimes the pieces, such as at Dartington, can be difficult to identify. Occasionally such new seats were not for the laity but for the clergy or readers. This happened at Thornbury when the screen was pulled down. Some pieces were retained to be used for new choir stalls as were parts of the bench ends.[202]

Left: *Churchstanton's gallery.*
Right: *A bench end incorporated into Stoke Rivers' pulpit.*

Designs of bench ends

Early design may have been led initially in the 1400s, if not earlier, from Exeter Cathedral and from the major monastic houses and churches. Craftsmen can be seen at this time moving between the major churches.

It may not be insignificant that in 1491 the church at Bodmin, Cornwall's county town, chose to emulate the carved seats already in place at the priory church at Plympton St Mary.[203] Later local men did much of Devon's church work. For example, in 1593 the parishioners of Northam gave the contract for rebuilding the north aisle of their church to two local men, Richard Browne of Abbotsham and Edward Browne of Bideford.

Colebrooke's unfinished bench end and the plain ends at Coldridge.

By this date churchwardens' accounts only record indigenous craftsmen being employed in the variety of rebuilding and maintenance work.[204] It is, as will be explained in the pages that follow, more difficult to determine who was responsible for the earlier woodwork.

Devon has a variety of styles and designs in its bench ends. A considerable number have simple plain ends. Some can be found at Honeychurch, Clovelly and Welcombe while nearly entire churches are filled with them at Cookbury and Parracombe St Petrock as well as Hartland.[205] The north aisle of Coldridge is also lined with plain benches. These parishes might not have been able to afford elaborate carving or the seats might have been designated for poorer parishioners. The plain style may also have been preferred. There are two plain bench ends at Colebrooke but

one of them is, on closer examination, simply unfinished. A portion of the bench was carved and the scratched lines of the discontinued carving can be clearly seen on the panel. One local tradition explains this was due to the joiner not being paid for his work.[206]

Nearly all of Devon's medieval bench ends are more ornately carved and this extends not merely to the central panel but also to its borders. These are occasionally plain

Above: Braunton.   *Right:* Coldridge.

and some, notably Broadwoodwidger, have very light if not elementary carving on the borders. Coldridge and Sutcombe have very elegant and simple borders. Most benches have foliate designs along the edges and in some churches each end has a different border. Those at Dunchideock in particular have been suggested to be based on seaweed but this is observational speculation rather than based on any firm evidence.[207] Pancrasweek is another parish church which has unusual borders: one of its two surviving bench ends has shields carved within the foliage design. The most strikingly carved are at Ashcombe. In this church the 38 bench ends have a simple Gothic tracery of two tiers with between two and four arches. The borders are the principal feature. Each has differing foliate designs but a handful feature creatures of the night including a newt, a frog, several snakes, a greater number of fallen angels and a few tortured faces and unknown creatures. Miss Beatrix Feodore Clara Augusta Grace Cresswell, illustrious in name at least, must have forgotten Ashcombe's bench ends when she gave those at Mortehoe the accolade of being 'the most nightmare-like creatures'.[208]

The Ashcombe collection is unique in and to Devon. New seats were built in the church in 1614 and further work paid for in 1618 but not enough money was expended to suggest that all 38 could have been carved in those years. It is likely the early seventeenth-century seats were additional to an existing scheme. In

One of the demonic creatures at Ashcombe.

A fallen angel at Ashcombe.

100

A corner figure at Ashcombe.

Another of the disturbing figures at Ashcombe.

Tortured faces at Ashcombe.

An Ashcombe angel.

One of Combe-in-Teignhead's unusual borders.

Two figures at Payhembury.

1641 the 'parson's pew' was built but this is unlikely to have been part of this set.[209] It is probable the benches were carved in the sixteenth or fifteenth centuries. In the mid 1800s the Exeter Diocesan Architectural Society described them as 'being of very superior description'.[210] A useful comparison with Ashcombe is with the handful of bench ends that have survived at Combe-in-Teignhead. These also have unusual borders but they have particular interest in figures at their bases: various cavorting beasts share the edges with human heads, one of which has sprouting foliage from his mouth.

Devon's carved borders are not as common in Somerset or Dorset where the edges tend to be plain. However, there is a strong similarity with Cornwall where the borders are elaborate and the decoration runs only along the Devon boundary and westward through to Cornwall.

Payhembury, Thornbury and Abbotsham are distinguished by unusual carving in the base panels. Payhembury has two heads placed within foliage and interestingly the carver set within top foils other motifs such as a bow & arrows and a bird astride what might be a faggot of wood. Thornbury is different again in that it has three faces on its reused bench ends: there is, like Payhembury, another foliage face, a woman with a close-fitting cap and a man with a magnificent Old Testament beard. What makes these carvings intriguing is not merely that the two parishes are unusual in having designed their benches in this way but that they are located in the far east and west of Devon.

102

An unusual design at Payhembury.

One of Thornbury's portraits.

Abbotsham, in the far north, is different again with the most imaginative use of the base panels in any Devon church: faces and dogs feature as incidental details but other carving is integral to the overall design.

Devon's benches appear to have originally been kept as bare wood and some were later painted such as at Lustleigh.[211] The remnants of those in the porch at George Nympton still have paint as do all of Churchstanton's

103

Dowland's painted bench ends.

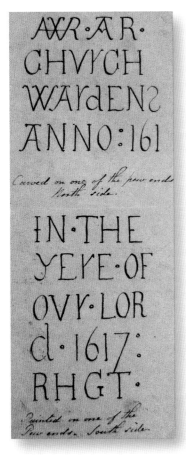

AXR·AR·
CHVYCH
WARdENS
ANNO:161

Carved on one of the pew ends North side.

IN·THE
YEYE·OF
OVY·LOR
d·1617:
RHGT·

Painted in one of the Pew ends. South side.

ends. Another exception is Dowland where letters were originally finely painted in black paint on a few bench ends *(left)*. On one end paint was applied to accentuate the light carving of the letters and numbers. Another deviation from this was in the church of Ashford. A drawing was made in the nineteenth century of two bench ends, neither of which now exist, on which one was carved 'AXR AR CHURCH WARDENS ANNO 161' but on the other was painted 'IN THE YERE OF OUR LORD 1617 RH GH'. The two initials were presumably of other churchwardens. Some churches to the east in Somerset, such as Bishops Lydeard, used paint within the background of the main design but Devon appears to have largely refrained from this. Some Cornish bench ends of this date were also painted but this was done mainly, although not exclusively, to show heraldry[212] and at Talland in south-east Cornwall the occupiers' names were painted in delicate lettering.

Dowland's painting is part of the tradition of identifying benches with their owners and this could be achieved by four different means. Coats of arms, initials, names and pictorial depictions were all employed to designate ownership of seats.

Carved heraldry on the ends may have been the preferred means for families who could sport a coat of arms. Approximately a third of Devon's churches with bench ends have shields with coats of arms and devices. Angels are proudly presenting these at Buckland Monachorum, East Budleigh, Kenton, Woodbury, Huntsham and North Tawton amongst other places. The heraldry could indicate the patron of the church as well as the family who owned the rights to the seats.

Above: Painted bench ends at St Breward and Bishop's Lydeard.

105

Left (clockwise): Angels at Kenton, North Tawton, Buckland Monachorum and Huntsham.

Amongst the families whose heraldry is depicted are the Raleighs at East Budleigh, the Grenvilles at Bideford, the Staffords at Dolton and the Bourchiers at Tawstock. Horwood has those of the Pollard, Trevelyan and Cockworthy families.[213] Weare Giffard has both the arms of the Fortescues on one bench end and the crescent and mullet of the Denzell family on another end panel with their rampant lion.[214] The carver at East Budleigh created two shields which are represented as having been partly unrolled, thereby indicating it was not made of wood but of paper or cloth. Interestingly, the shields are not held by angels but by a man on one bench and by a woman on the other. The two seats adjoin one another and clearly relate to each other.

Other benches use a rebus, the symbol which denoted a family. In several Churston Ferrers and Bere Ferrers bench ends can be seen that of the Ferrers family, the horseshoe. The Bourchier Knot is on bench ends across Devon. It is more widely known as the Reef Knot. Alwington, Ashford, Cheldon, Dowland, Landcross, Monkleigh, Powderham Castle Chapel, Rewe, Roborough, Sutcombe and Weare Giffard churches all have examples on bench ends. The family's home parish, Tawstock, also has the knot carved on the end of a seat.

Heraldry at Ashcombe.

A Bourchier knot at Roborough.

One of the heraldic shields at Alwington.

Bouche shields
at Feniton.

An unusual set of initials on two
levels at Weare Giffard.

Blank shields were also placed on bench ends. This might have been seen as merely decorative or possibly they were once temporarily painted with names of individuals or tenements. Occasionally, notably at Feniton, Stockleigh Pomeroy and Braunton, the craftsmen carved a bouche shield. These have a notch along one side and originally indicated where a knight placed his lance.

Initials are the most common means of identifying owners. Individuals, probably mostly those without coats of arms, placed their initials on the bench ends. An exception to this can be seen at Weare Giffard where the Fortescue's coat of arms is carved but

Elaborate carving of the letter N at Buckland Filleigh.

Another example of the Buckland Filleigh carvings.

Marwood's distinctive style of depicting letters.

'George C' at Rewe.

below it lies the initials of Bartholomew Fortescue and his wife Ellen. At Buckland Filleigh the lettering is particularly finely carved and emulates leather or metal-work. Marwood has some of the oddest examples as the initials were carved sideways and upside down. Here the lettering is also ornate with graceful Gothic lines. It has been suggested that the similar upside-down letters at Braunton were caused by the carver being illiterate: J. C. D. Smith, an authority on carving, speculated that the craftsman worked from drawings but did not know which way the letters should face. Another writer questioned whether it indicated humility in the seat holder.[215] Weare Giffard has the distinction of having a shield carved with not just one set of initials but under each is a secondary pair. Possibly these were later holders of the seat who wanted their ownership noted. A much more limited number of bench ends have names carved. Rewe has two such benches: on one is carved 'George C.' while the other has 'George Col & Jone h[is] w[iwfe]'.[216] Coldridge has a bench with a re-carved inscription of the early 1500s. There is also a merchant's mark at Braunton and possibly another at Whimple.

Whimple.

109

Village art

More difficult to decipher are the pictorial representations which are outside the two main styles, Gothic and the Renaissance, that permeate Devon's bench ends. In 1917 two respected authorities noticed there were carvings 'of human interest'.

Left: Abbotsham's man riding backward.
Below: *The would-be bishop and prior at Frithelstock.*

Nikolaus Pevsner might also have had bench ends in mind when he referred to Cornish slate memorials as *Volkskunst*, Folk Art.[217] A less whimsical term might be Village Art. These carvings were local in nature and did not come from outside influences but rather were representations generated from within an immediate area and with a known meaning and significance. At this time screens, pulpits, fonts and glass were media that rarely represented parishioners or scenes of everyday life. Only church monuments, and occasionally glass, were used to represent local people. These bench end carvings are akin to the tradition of those misericords which drew inspiration from local experiences. The carver would have known the people that he was representing on the end of his bench. They had meaning within the village.

Even so, the significance behind some carvings has often been lost after four centuries or more. This has led to speculation by subsequent generations of parishioners: at Sandford it has been conjectured that their carvings are of Aztecs, in Frithelstock two heads have been supposed to be

111

One of the unusual carvings at East Budleigh.

the bishop of Exeter sticking his tongue out at the prior, the carving of a man riding backwards at Abbotsham has been suggested to represent a Christian wasting his chance in attacking evil, and the rector of Northlew wondered if a rose and *fleur-de-lys* on his bench ends indicated the craftsmen were English and French.[218] Historians have also been at a loss to explain the woodwork: one writer thought the Bideford panels were portions of Flemish furniture brought over by local sailors.[219]

One of Devon's most striking Village Art bench end carvings is of a domestic scene at East Budleigh. A woman is shown standing at a counter or country door. A dressed animal hangs to her right. She holds a trencher with one hand and the tail of a dog with the other. The meaning is uncertain but it may be that the animal is a turnspit dog, bred to turn the wheel of a kitchen spit.

Another end has a woman eating what might be a chicken drumstick. There is a seat with a maritime theme. A vessel is prominently displayed in the centre. It appears to be in

A woman eating a chicken drumstick at East Budleigh.

dock, two men are in the rigging, a castle lies in the background and a skiff is in the foreground. This has long been assumed to be the seat of a ship-owner. Behind the first row of gentry seats is a bench whose end is carved with what appears to be a merchant's emblems. An angel holds a shield on which has been placed cloth shears. Above them are teasels, the flower heads which were used in the making of woollen cloth. These have confused observers

East Budleigh's mixture of unusual carvings.

but the image is similar to others in Cullompton and Tiverton which have been conclusively shown to be teasels.[220] Another end in the church features the coat of arms of the Dennis family and beneath it lies a pair of scissors and a long animal biting his tail. This has been suggested to be a sheep but interestingly a similar figure was carved at Lakenheath in Suffolk which has been thought to be a self-castrating beaver (in order to save his life from hunters seeking his glands which were thought to have medicinal properties).[221]

Further east is yet another unusual collection albeit much smaller. The former Devon parish of Churchstanton, now in Somerset, has

Churchstanton's distinctive collection of bench ends.

31 bench-ends most of which form the front of the west gallery. They may have been made when the church was re-seated in 1564.[222] Davidson visited the church in 1828 and found them 'very curious'. He also noted the variety of design but also that many were in 'a decaying condition'.[223] Two years later the seats were destroyed and the ends reused for the gallery. It was probably at this time that they were painted mustard yellow which obscures the workmanship but even so the fineness of the carving is self-evident. This is a collection unlike any other in Devon. Many bench ends have Gothic diaper patterns but there are four others which are not in the tradition of other Devon bench end carving. The most striking is of a male figure, dressed in a cloak, clasping two staffs. The figures on the church's bench ends are no longer those of Chaucer's England but of Shakespeare's, in effect there has been a transition from the medieval period to the Elizabethan. The Renaissance also flows

115

Farming at Thorverton.

Bickleigh near Tiverton, Clayhanger, Stockleigh Pomeroy and Abbotsham.

through the carving along with improbable birds as well as several animals. The main figure is clearly symbolic of an individual or even of a social position in the parish.

A farmer might be indicated at Thorverton where the carving has a harrow, plough and shovel. Nearby at Bickleigh is a walking figure carrying a bag of tools but his occupation is unclear. Clayhanger has a male figure holding a spade and Stockleigh Pomeroy has another man with what looks like a walking stick, a shepherd's crook? Abbotsham is more straightforward: on one bench are carved the tools of a woodworker: a scalpel, a hammer, dividing compass and a carpenter's square are shown on two shields.

A figure of death is also at Abbotsham but part of him has been worn or cut away. St Braddock in Cornwall

Above – left to right:
Abbotsham, Marwood, Tavistock
and Down St Mary.
Below – left to right:
Landcross and Bodmin in
Cornwall.

has a more complete Grim Reaper who holds his scythe in one hand and a head (not a skull) in the other. Entertainers are more common in Devon. Abbotsham also has what might be a tumbler. There is a bagpipe player at Marwood and another at Tavistock on a section of wood that is possibly too large to be a bench end.

Some of the most unusual must be the contortionists at Landcross. On two bench ends two separate figures squeeze themselves into constricted spaces. A similar individual is at Abbotsham and another is at Bodmin in Cornwall but, unlike those in Devon, he has his right hand reaching up his backside. There is a mermaid at

Above – left to right:
Braunton, Clayhanger, Landcross and Down St Mary.

Down St Mary, a hunting scene at Braunton and what could be fools throughout Devon. Finally, if images signify the seat-holder, then it becomes mystifying why one seat in Clayhanger has a harpy.

It could reasonably be assumed that in many parishes the person(s) paying for the seat, whether the churchwardens or occupiers, agreed with the joiners on the overall design. This may have been a compromise between what could be afforded and with what could be technically achieved. An incomplete design on the inside of a bench end at Broadwoodwidger was not followed through to the other. The two designs are radically different and perhaps whoever was responsible for the carving was unhappy with what was being offered.

It would be reasonable to also believe that designs had meaning for the occupier. The parish church of Monkleigh has today a handful of ancient carved

Left: A Victorian drawing of the Romayne Heads at Down St Mary.

118

Left: Lapford.
Right: Thornbury.
Below: High Bickington.

benches. In about 1641 a new seating plan was arranged for the church and this presumably had occurred several generations after the seats had been erected. It was remembered in 1691 that temporary tickets or notes were fixed to the seats to indicate which properties related to each seat.[224] The visual representation was either not strong enough or the meanings had been lost. Across Devon are many Renaissance medallions with profiles of both men and women. Countless viewers have speculated on whether these were the images of the occupiers or merely standard representations of people of their time.

Devon has two main types of carving: Gothic and Renaissance imagery permeate the bench ends. There is a wide dispersal of these styles alongside some notable geographical patterns. Devon's craftsmen also used religious symbols to further embellish their carving.

119

Gothic

Gothic design dominates Devon's bench ends. This was no doubt due to the rebuilding or enlargement of so many local churches taking place in the late fifteenth century when the Perpendicular period was at its height. The elements of the Gothic period are widespread: tracery, foliage and geometric patterns are in every corner of Devon.

Tracery

Gothic arches can be found on Devon's church doors, fonts, pulpits, screens, monuments and seating as well as in the windows. The earliest depiction of a Devon bench end

shows Gothic tracery: a panel of stained glass at Doddiscombsleigh (*far left*), thought to have been made at Exeter in the 1470s, illustrates a priest sitting on a bench carved with a single arch of one round foil.

It may not be surprising that with this prevalence of Gothic tracery that a significant number of churches have bench ends with only 'blank' tracery, that is, no decoration other than the tracery. However, what is astonishing is that these buildings are all in southern Devon. The only exception is Atherington which is also unusual for its poppy heads. The latter has arches with creative designs, not only is each bench end different but the patterns are inventive in the use of tracery. Twenty-five of Devon's 123 churches with surviving bench ends are limited to plain Gothic tracery.[225] Some Ottery St Mary benches, with some notable exceptions, also have blank Gothic tracery but like most churches there is a mixture of other design.

EXMOOR

DEVON

Atherington

Coldridge

Bickleigh

Plymtree

Talaton

Colebrooke

Cheriton Bishop

Whimple

South Tawton

Drewsteignton

Tedburn St Mary

EXETER

Dunchideock

Kenn

Christow

Woodbury

Ashton

Powderham

DARTMOOR

Chudleigh

Ashcombe

East Ogwell

Buckland Monachorum

Broadhempston

Bere Ferrers

Dartington

Stoke Gabriel

PLYMOUTH

Kingston

Churches dominated by
Gothic tracery

Nymet Rowland.

Colebrooke.

The bench ends with restrained Gothic arches are located in three small groups: one collection runs from Stoke Gabriel to East Ogwell, another from Chudleigh through to the west of Crediton and finally another group lies in and around

Ottery St Mary. The remaining Devon churches, with the exception of Bere Ferrers, Buckland Monachorum and Kingston, have more elaborate carving. There is no other such concentration of plain tracery in east Cornwall[226] but

Bere Ferrers.

Coldridge.

it continues into Dorset and south Somerset. Wambrook, formerly Devon but now Somerset, has only blank Gothic tracery as do the parishes south of Taunton.

Many of the carvers aimed for uniformity when working with blank tracery. The bench ends at Bere Ferrers and in the neighbouring parish of Buckland Monachorum are interesting in this respect. Each bench in the former church has the same design except for three

Stoke Gabriel.

Cheriton Bishop.

which have coats of arms. The only other differences between them are in the form of the columns that intrude into the arcades. Close inspection reveals slight changes in the execution of the design.

There are great variations in Gothic tracery. Some benches have a simple single arch while most have between two and five. Many ends have arches with two tiers. It is most common to find double arches on

125

two tiers with each arch having a trefoil. Others are more elaborate and mimic the changes in style from the Early English period of architecture of the thirteenth century through the Decorated Period of the fourteenth century and finally to the most elaborate of the fifteenth century. Coldridge and Modbury are examples of more sophisticated carving. The single surviving bench end at Drewsteignton is elegant and refined while there are many others in Devon which are more rustic in comparison particularly such as those at Honeychurch and Nymet Rowland. The seats in these two churches are similar in the simplicity of their carving. It is likely that workmen introduced new styles to churches and became inventive in mixing older forms: many other Devon churches use Gothic tracery as a basic structure to their design and then fuse other elements. The tracery patterns provided a visual counterpoint for their occupants: the carvings were in the line of vision with the windows above them. The occupant's gaze would also have taken in Gothic tracery in its other forms throughout the church notably the screens which Devon specialised in. The majority of Devon's other bench ends use Gothic tracery combined with other traditional Gothic elements.

Foliage and geometry

Foliage and geometric patterns are another hallmark of the Gothic style. Two parishes some twenty miles apart are each dominated by foliate design. Tetcott has a few

Bondleigh.

bench ends carved with simple geometric foliage above open arches. These are rudimentary, described as uncouth in 1849,[227] and similar to those at Bondleigh which are perhaps more accomplished but are still open and yet

Tetcott.

St Winnow in Cornwall.

elegantly carved. Tetcott sits along the Cornish border and no other church in this area is dominated as it is with these simple foliage design although there is a similar carving at Laneast and another like it at St Winnow near Fowey.

Devon's surviving collections of ancient benches usually include foliate design to some extent. In many these are worked into Gothic tracery. At West Worlington the plant motifs are more pronounced and form the

127

West Worlington.

Northleigh.

greater part of the design including even the cusps of
the tracery. At Northleigh delicate daisy-like flowers rise
up on over-long stems which form the vertical lines of
the tracery. In other churches, such as Hatherleigh and
occasionally at North Tawton, the foliage is over-size and
fills the bench ends with leaves.

Some plants assumed stiff geometric patterns
that sit alongside the foils of various shapes. Devon
carvers used another Gothic feature in that these foliage
and geometric motifs were repeated as a 'diaper' pattern.
These tend to be symmetrical. West Worlington has
bold but intricate carving with the plants in some bench
ends just as uniform as the geometric patterns also
deployed in the same or neighbouring benches. There are
strong similarities in nearby Puddington but the overall
symmetrical diaper design is offset in one carved end by a
different and contrasting motif. The inventiveness of the
carver shines through his woodwork. Flowers and plants
also dominate at Venn Ottery near Sidmouth where
foliage fills the tracery on one bench end. Like other
places, Churston Ferrers has carving where the foliage
is separated by geometric patterns. Also like many other
churches, the flowers and foliage are imaginary and were
not intended to be accurate representations of known
plants. This may be in contrast to the two Christow
bench ends which have plants similar to pomegranates.

Right: Hatherleigh.

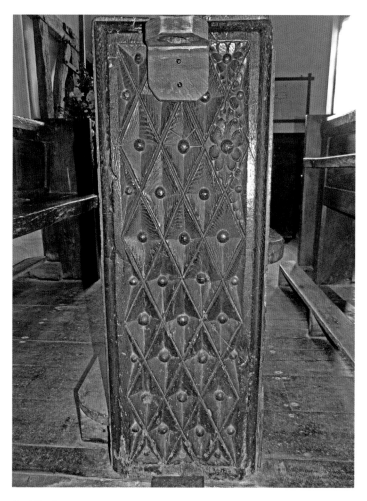

Puddington.

Venn Ottery.

Devon's foliate carving is different in this respect from neighbouring Somerset where the species of plants can be more readily identified.

    Exceptional diaper pattern can be found in

Ottery St Mary. Here the carving is imaginative and surprising. Each bench uses tracery and mixes geometric and foliate shapes with the exception of one bench end which has a three-stemmed flowering plant rising out

Christow.

Ottery St Mary.

of a ewer. That design is reminiscent of one bench end at Marwood and particularly of carvings throughout neighbouring Somerset. The benches at Ottery St Mary are exceptionally well-carved and are to be found in the

Dorset Aisle where they may have been re-sited in the nineteenth century. In 1869 the vicar questioned whether they were the remnant of the church's seats from 1645 when Parliament's soldiers occupied the church during

131

Left and Above: *Ottery St Mary.*

Marwood.

the Civil War. Reverend Cornish speculated that they were moved to make room for the men and that others were used for fuel. The church was subsequently filled with high pews.[228]

In many churches there is a mix of Gothic tracery, foliage and geometric motifs. Some carvings in each church are highly reminiscent of others across Devon but closer examination shows they are not identical.

133

Renaissance

Renaissance motifs were introduced into Devon by the generation preceding the Reformation with the earliest recorded work possibly at Landcross in 1503 which would make it a very early date for its introduction into England. Alternatively, the date could be 1552, if the carver's familiarity with Roman letters was as poor as it might have been, which would make it much less remarkable.

Left: Sutcombe and Northlew.
Below: Lapford.

Renaissance elements were sometimes married with Gothic forms with the result that bench ends acquired a new diversity in their patterns. Renaissance imagery does not have the implied meaning of religious motifs. These new forms were purely decorative and secular and as such could have been intended to remove themselves from potential contemporary questions about images being perceived as idolatrous.

In the early 1500s the great period of church rebuilding was underway in Devon and Gothic features predominated when the Renaissance arrived. Some churches had already erected seats with Gothic design. This may be why few Devon parish churches have purely Renaissance elements in its seating. Lapford and Down St Mary, situated to the north of Crediton, have some good Renaissance work but they also retain their Gothic structures. Both place Renaissance images on shields that are situated between Gothic tracery at the top and foils at the base.

This could be the work of the same carpenter. A century ago Miss Prideaux commented that if the shields were removed there would be no difference between these benches and those from the Perpendicular period of the Gothic movement. Lapford, she wrote, has 'the characteristic union of these Renaissance details with purely Gothic forms and workmanship'.[229] Likewise, the benches at Northlew use shields for the same purpose and this device can also be seen elsewhere such as at Sutcombe. In 1915 Miss Prideaux noted the carvings in that church and observed that the 'asp, amphisbena, dragons of all kinds, fish, hairy men, mermen, goats, serpents, a griffin and a sheep all figure in this motley array, besides grotesque human heads of surpassing hideousness arrayed in headdresses of equally exaggerated character'.[230]

The Renaissance figures are similar to the earlier misericord carvings of imaginary animals and as difficult to interpret. As long ago as 1125 St Bernard of Clairvaux asked:

'What mean those ridiculous monstrosities in the courts of cloisters; those filthy apes, those fierce lions, those monstrous centaurs, those half-men, those spotted tigers, those fighting soldiers and horn-blowing hunters; many bodies under one head, or many heads on one body; here a serpent's tail attached to a quadruped, there a quadruped's head on a fish; here a beast presenting the foreparts of a horse, and dragging after it the rear of a goat; there a horned animal with the hind parts of a horse?' [231]

His question is equally applicable to the Renaissance carvings in Devon.

The carving at Newton St Petrock, between Holsworthy and Bideford, is similar to Sutcombe but the joiner also discarded Gothic convention in other seats and filled his end panels solely with Renaissance design. He repeatedly carved variations of a creature that blended human, animal and foliage forms in unnatural combinations. This 'grotesque' was a feature common in Renaissance design but his creation had an eel-like body with tendrils that sprout forth out of his mouth. His long, thin delicate form swirls about the bench end and sometimes he, or possibly even she, is a bearded figure. Other Devon carvers provide a fuller body for their version of this Renaissance grotesque and some carving indicates scales or feathers. All are fanciful and unnatural creations with a lack of hostility. There is an elegance if not a slight sense of humour. These figures cannot be termed Christian and are seemingly as out of place in a church as the earlier Gothic gargoyles are to modern eyes. There is also a balance to the forms and many are symmetrical. Each appears to develop if not evolve in various permutations as they rise and wriggle from below. Miss Cresswell regarded one collection of these grotesques as 'a whole collection of creatures such as never went into the ark'. She also scoffed at the church guide which claimed one figure on a Tawstock bench end was a hunky-punk, an imaginary malevolent creature. In Miss Cresswell's opinion the carving was simply a typical Renaissance monster.[232]

Westleigh.

Newton St Petrock.

Tawstock.

Westleigh.

The Renaissance's other designs are equally inventive, flamboyant and nonsensical. There are full-bodied cupids, often wingless and generally nude, who occasionally play instruments. Stockleigh Pomeroy's cupids are particularly well fed in the face. Another feature of the Renaissance are Romayne Heads, the profiles of men and women presented within medallions. Some share a bench end and directly face one another with shapes coming out of their mouths reminiscent of medieval green men. These protrudences could be tendrils or might have indicated speech or music. At North Bovey one such man has beads pouring from his mouth. Many men have fantastic hats and often there are exaggerated beards. One at Sandford has what could be imagined to be a pipe in his mouth.

Sandford church has a number of striking portraits. Two have hair which could indicate they had African origins or equally that they were modelled on Bacchus. One young girl has pigtails. This is a substantial set of bench ends with a character of its own but like those of East Budleigh they refrained from the use of religious imagery.

Left: *Stockleigh Pomeroy.*
Above right: *Sandford.*
Bottom row:
Left: *Littleham near Bideford.*
Centre: *Sandford.*
Right: *Sandford.*

Sandford. *Sandford.* *Sandford.* *Westleigh.*

The carver ignored Gothic design except for geometric foliage: one lone bench end has Gothic tracery. The location of these bench ends in close proximity to Renaissance carving in the screens at Lapford and Morchard Bishop, as well as to the benches at Lapford and Down St Mary, raises questions as to whether workmen or patrons found the same inspiration.

Another figure that can be seen in a great number of churches is that of a male face set within foliage: Bideford, Clayhanger, Dowland, East Budleigh, High Bickington, Landcross, Newton St Petrock, Sandford and Westleigh have particularly good examples of this Leaf Head. He differs from the concept of the Green Man in that he does not have tendrils sprouting from any orifice.

The best example of a Leaf Head is on what is perhaps the best known single bench end carving in Devon. At East Budleigh one such figure is locally known as the Red Indian and has been identified as such by English Heritage.[233] He has been branded a Native American because of the resident gentry family, the Raleighs. If the bench was carved at the same time as the Raleigh seat, 1534, then it would have been erected more than a full generation before Native Americans were known to have visited Devon. Its apparent feather headdress is revealed, on close inspection, to be leaves. The figure's prominent nose has also won over devotees to the American identification but little attention has ever been given to his leaf beard, a feature not common to early Americans.

High Bickington.

East Budleigh.

High Bickington.

Transitional carvings from Gothic to Renaissance can be found across Devon but are particularly strong in North Devon. The complexity of deciphering design is aptly illustrated by the collection at Alwington, another church near Bideford. The benches which are in situ deploy Gothic design and these were probably built for the church. Others form bench front panels and backs as well as part of the reredos and pulpit but these are very different: they deploy a mixture of Gothic and Renaissance motifs. One

141

A typical North Devon Renaissance man.

East Budleigh.   *Bideford.*

explanation could be that these two sets of bench ends were carved at different periods but church records prove that bench ends were acquired from nearby Parkham church and these were used to embellish Alwington. Those which still serve as bench ends were original to the church while the others were part of this acquisition some two hundred years ago. Alwington's history is easily understood because the church records are detailed.[234] It is impossible to understand so readily the histories of other churches because of the paucity of their written evidence.

Landcross, also in North Devon, has a collection with no parallels. It retains a limited use of Gothic tracery and geometric foliage. Like elsewhere there are portraits but there are two motifs which are unusual and one which will not be found outside the church. One of these curious designs, as discussed earlier, is on two separate bench ends. These depict individual figures, each squeezed within his or her own arch. They might be meant to be contortionists. A similar motif can be seen nearby at Abbotsham. The other interesting image is on two shields on one bench end. This seat has two angel-like figures with great batwings. Each is depicted as if made of string and their feet have tassels. One is at prayer.

Tawstock also has a small number of bench ends with delicately carved Renaissance design. Gothic Tracey is forgotten here. Their execution is similar to those from Parkham (but now at Alwington). Likewise there is a collection of panels with rich Renaissance carving which

Top row, left: Landcross.
Top row, centre and right: Bideford.
Botom row: Bideford.

now forms the tower screen at Bideford. These have been suggested to have been the original bench ends from the church[235] and if so would have made for incredible viewing. Many are portraits set within square frames and would appear to have been originally carved with some Gothic design. When James Davidson, the East Devon antiquarian,

143

Fighting cocks at Powderham Castle.

visited the church in 1848 he described the reader's desk as having the same style of carving.[236] The tower screen may have originated from several sources.

Many churches have a mix of Gothic tracery, foliate and Renaissance designs but it is at Littleham near Bideford that Gothic elements have almost entirely disappeared.[237] There is some transitional tracery using new motifs. The carving is a great leap forward from earlier designs: foliage creatures are part of the arcading as well as being the dominant focal points in many of the bench ends.

Miss Prideaux was one of the first to comment on the Renaissance influence on Devon's bench ends design. She noted of the aforementioned Lapford's carvings that they were semi-pagan but appreciated the beauty of the carving of the border of one end. In her opinion the freedom, vigour and grace expressed in the work was in each instance equally remarkable.[238] Much the same could be said of one of the most surprising collections in Devon. Powderham Castle Chapel has eight bench ends thought to have been taken from South Huish Church. The carvings are among the most imaginative in Devon. Figures have exaggerated sleeves and hats but several have impossibly long necks to go with them. Alongside them are fantastic creatures as well as a pair of fighting cocks and below them a pair of dragons similarly engaged in battle.[239] In 1841 James Davidson found ancient benches at South Huish but he described these as being 'carved in

Two females with unusual headress at Powderham Castle.

trefoil headed panels'.[240] His description fails to capture the essence of the carved wood now at Powderham Castle and it may be that they originated from another church. They differ from those in the parish church at Powderham and the style of carving is also dissimilar to the Renaissance bench ends in North Devon's churches where there is a shared style in the motifs which are placed on shields within Gothic tracery. The Powderham benches, once located as they were possibly deep within the South Hams, were executed with different motifs. Unlike other Devon bench ends these divide the panel into two halves with two separate designs. The carving is not fine but has flair and elegance if not lightness to it. The lack of other Renaissance bench end carving in the South Hams poses the question of what there might have been in these other neighbouring churches.

Religious images

Religious carvings form a significant part of the designs on many Devon benches. Their variety and distinctiveness have been unappreciated as has their geographical pattern.

A diverse range of religious motifs was carved on shields, a standard design format since the thirteenth century.[241] Some images are unusual, such as the hand holding rosary beads at Ashwater and High Bickington has a saint who appears to hold a rosary. Somerset has at least three churches with similar carvings.[242] A much more common motif in Devon is that of a saint. Many have been defaced but the rest of their bodies are nearly always intact. High Bickington, Horwood and Monkleigh have good examples of saints but they also occur in parishes in the south (Combe-in-Teignhead), the west (Lewtrenchard), the east (Yarcombe) and particularly throughout the north. One that was near Plymouth, at Plympton St Maurice, was destroyed in 1870: it was recorded shortly afterwards that 'the last remaining bench end, containing a rudely-carved figure of a saint holding a cross, was got rid of'. [243]

Some saints can be identified by their symbols, such as St James at High Bickington. His shell is noticeably depicted on his hat. It may be St Paul who was carved on a bench end now at Powderham Castle Chapel: he holds a book and sword. The carving of St Brannoc at Braunton is one of the best known in Devon. He has a bullock in the bottom panel. St Michael is on a bench end at Lewtrenchard and holds his scales whilst standing above his dragon. The saints at Combe-in-Teignhead are well-preserved although there are uncertainties

Left: *Ashwater.*
Below: *Yarcombe.*

147

St James at Yarcombe.

St James at High Bickington.

St Paul with his sword and book at Powderham.

St Brannock at Braunton.

Marwood.

High Bickington.

St John at Weare Giffard.

A Marian symbol at Ashwater.

The head of John the Baptist at Coldridge.

Lewtrenchard's depiction of Christ?

The Crucifixion at West Woolfardisworthy.

about their identities.[244] The head of St John the Baptist can be found in a number of churches including Coldridge, Weare Giffard, Lewtrenchard and Braunton. These are a portion of the 50 saints' images found in Devon's bench ends.[245]

Marian symbols were carved for such churches as Ashwater, Braunton, Broadwoodwidger, Sutcombe and West Woolfardisworthy. This symbol is a monogram in which can be read each of the letters of the Virgin's name. In some churches the letter M is crowned. Yarcombe also has the Virgin Mary holding the baby Jesus.

There are fewer images of Christ. Lewtrenchard and Broadwoodwidger have the same full-length figure, without a halo, who appears to be giving the benediction. There are also two crucifixions at West Woolfardisworthy and Abbotsham. At the latter church the faces of Mary and John were cut away while that of Jesus was removed and then reinserted. Close observation reveals careful restoration.[246] There are also carvings which indicate Christ in other ways. Shields with the initials IHS

149

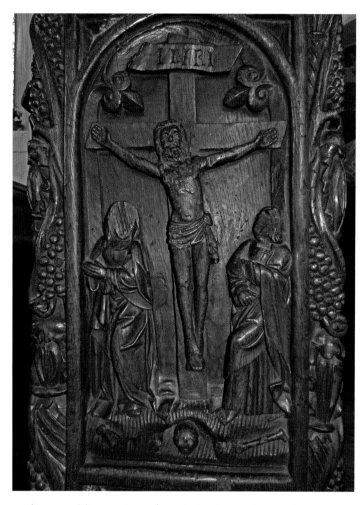

Above: *IHC at Buckland Filleigh.*
Left: *The crufixion with the replaced head of Jesus today, and an early drawing at Abbotsham.*

and IHC, abbreviations for Christ in the Greek language, can be found in churches such as Abbotsham, Braunton, Broadwoodwidger, Buckland Filleigh, Colebrooke, Frithelstock, Northlew, Powderham Castle Chapel and West Woolfardisworthy.

A great number of hearts appear on bench ends. Many have been notched, such as one at Newton St Petrock, which is meant to signify the piercing of Jesus' heart by the Roman soldier's spear. Hatherleigh has three notched hearts carved in the base panel of a bench end. Ashwater has the Sacred Heart of Jesus shining with divine light, a heart with flames emanates from it. Across from it is a shield with a crown above a rose, an image which is commonly interpreted as Marian. Other hearts have less obvious meanings and help illustrate the difficulties of interpretation. The unusual collection of bench ends at Whimple, noted in the mid nineteenth

Hatherleigh.

Whimple.

Doddiscombsleigh.

Marwood.

century to have been 'restored and copied in the nave',[247] includes three shields with hearts pierced by one, two and four arrows. Doddiscombsleigh also has a pierced heart. Northlew has four bench ends with hearts. One is on a shield, a second is notched and on a plate, and a third has three arrows piercing it. At Marwood an inverted heart was placed near what might be a scroll or linen and another is grouped with a whip and what might be a torch.

The most commonly depicted heart is part of the *Arma Christi,* the instruments of the Passion. Some 150 carvings can be seen in twenty-three parish churches.[248] Nearly every one is located in North Devon. They are centred around Bideford but run north to Mortehoe, south-westerly towards the Cornish border and in a

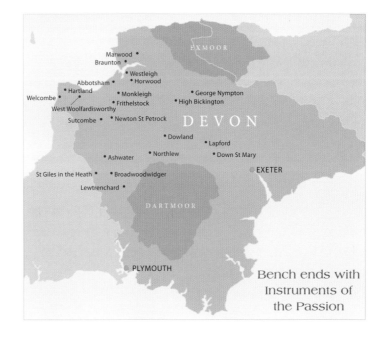

Bench ends with Instruments of the Passion

Left to Right: Lapford, Bridford, George Nympton and Newton St Petrock.

handful of parishes as far south-eastwards nearly to Crediton. The latter are three bench ends in the churches at Lapford and Down St Mary. Lapford has a shield with an unmistakeable image of the Passion: this shows the Five Wounds of Christ (the crucified hands and feet as well as his notched heart) and it would have been familiar to any churchgoer at the time of the Reformation and presumably for many years immediately afterwards. The two churches share a less recognisable image: a male figure holding a whip. These two figures most likely symbolised another of the instruments of the Passion. There is one other possible survival: Bridford Church has a shield with the Five Wounds. This is now part of a chair, which was constructed of old fragments and new wood in the early 1800s, but although the carving is ancient it may not necessarily be original to the church or part of a bench end.

By the late fifteenth century the Passion had assumed an importance in private and public devotion and has been described as taking a central role in worship for the generations before the Reformation.[249] Because of this it is curious that Passion carvings on benches are not found in the southern or eastern parts of Devon. This absence extends into Somerset which has few Passion carvings on bench ends, particularly with those churches that lie within twenty-five miles of the Devon boundary. In the parishes in the southern part of Somerset the emphasis is on blank Gothic tracery but there are fewer shields with any devices let alone those of the Passion. A dozen parishes lying in the immediate west of Bridgwater have another style: these bench ends favour foliate designs filling the end panel.

The Cornish bench ends along the Devon border are different. Cornwall has a higher proportion of churches with bench ends than Devon but a lower total number: some 80 of the 225 ancient churches have retained bench ends and there are a thousand bench ends in the eastern part of the county. The only sparse areas are to the west of Truro and in East Cornwall near Plymouth. In the northeast corner of Cornwall Gothic tracery dominates and with it there is a preponderance of shields. The symbols of the Passion are more common than they are in North Devon. There are more than double the number of Passion and other religious images in east Cornwall than there is in all of Devon. The themes are the same but the designs are not similar to Devon. This is surprising given four of the churches with bench ends, those of North Tamerton, North Petherwin, St Giles in the Heath and Broadwoodwidger, have been in both Devon and Cornwall as either civil or ecclesiastical parishes. The Cornish churches of Poughill and Launcells have remarkably similar carvings that suggest the same workmen. The Cornish churches not only used emblematic images of the Passion but depict Crucifixion events, a device not used in Devon. Other embellishments are unknown in Devon including a banner and the tomb of Jesus. There is also a shield that is hatched along the base. This is only found in Devon at Monkleigh. This corner of Cornwall also refrains from the depiction of saints, except for one bench end at Kilkhampton. Saints in North Devon are more common.

The Cornish Passion carvings are not restricted to the north coast: one of the largest Cornish collections is in Landulph, a parish which lies on the border with Devon directly across the Tamar from Bere Ferrers near Plymouth. The Passion carvings can be also found across Cornwall and their style changes westward. At St Braddock near Liskeard there is a small number and two are not found in Devon: on one shield are Four Wounds (the hands and feet of Jesus) while on another the pincers and hammer are depicted upside down.[250] At St Teath, between Tintagel and Padstow, the Virgin Mary's crowned monogram and the letters IHC dominate and

The four wounds at St Braddock in Cornwall.

Launcells in Cornwall with, on the right, the feet of Jesus ascending into heaven with his footprints left below him.

this is repeated with extraordinary regularity in the neighbouring parishes at St Endellion and Michaelstow.

East Devon and Dorset have few bench ends but a comparison between those that survive shows they share little in terms of common styles. The majority of Dorset's nine churches[251] with bench ends that are within twenty-five miles of Devon are along the Somerset border and have more in common with that county in terms of design. Wambrook, formerly Dorset and now Somerset, has Gothic tracery but four of the remaining benches are seventeenth century and Thorncombe, now Dorset, has linen-fold panels in its pulpit that might have been used for seating. No bench end in these churches has a depiction of the Passion.

The Passion locations prompt questions about their distribution pattern. Local tradition across Devon attributes the destruction of church furnishings to 'Cromwell', whether Thomas or Oliver, to unnamed Roundhead soldiers or to the Victorians. In 1909 it was believed in Braunton that 'during the Civil Wars some Puritan ruffians got in and proceeded to demolish the carved work with axes but were quickly ejected by the indignant parishioners before further damage was done'.[252] With regard to religious imagery, it may not be that religious images on bench ends were destroyed but that they may never have existed in south or east Devon. The geographic pattern could be the result of different cultures within the county. Was there a linked identity between Cornwall and the northern boundary parishes of Devon? [253]

It is possible that the Passion carvings' distribution relates to the reception and impact the Reformation had in Devon and be indicative of religious histories within parts of the South West. When Hugh Latimer came to Exeter in 1534 he found a mixed response to his Reformation preaching in the Cathedral Yard.[254] Three years before, in October 1531, Thomas Bennett had posted on the door of the cathedral his declaration that the pope was the Antichrist. He was tried for heresy and burned at the stake a few months later. Another discordant voice was that of Philip Gammon of Axminster who, a year after Latimer was in Exeter, said 'the blessing of a bishop was as good as the blessing of his old horse'. When a neighbour disagreed by pointing out that bishops were anointed with holy oil he replied there 'was as much virtue in the oil of a beast's foot as was in the oil that the bishop was anointed with'. Priests, he said, were 'all nought'.[255]

It is not possible to determine how Devonians viewed these first few years of the Reformation, with the dissolution of the religious houses in the 1530s, but the introduction of the Prayer Book resulted in a rebellion in 1549 that was of national importance. Its defeat ended with the deaths of many Devon followers including the hanging of the vicar of St Thomas from his own church tower. It was a symbolic move to execute him in his vestments and rosary beads but it is the rebels' own choice of symbol for their flag, that of the Five Wounds, that is of greater interest. The Pilgrimage of Grace in 1536 had also been accompanied by a similar flag and it may be that the Devon rebels had merely copied them.[256] Nevertheless, the use of that symbol must have been remembered by those other Devonians who sat in their parish benches looking across to their depictions of the Five Wounds. The Devon origins of the uprising was Sampford Courtenay, on the edge of where the Passion carvings can now be found.

An onlooker later wrote that the people of Exeter sympathised with the Prayer Book rebels and he suggested that this was widespread through the Devon countryside. It may be telling that after the Reformation there were many cases of defamation brought by clerics against their parishioners in the local church court. At Yealmpton a ballad was composed to publicise the illicit union of the vicar and a local woman. The parsons at West Alvington and Spreyton were both called whore-mongers by their parishioners. A rumour spread through Totnes that their vicar had danced drunk and naked in the streets one Saturday night in 1619. He had allegedly fallen and the injuries prevented him from conducting the service the next day. In Dawlish the vicar was accused of seducing wives and unmarried women as well as of attempted rape. There are more accusations against vicars recorded after the Reformation than in the years immediately before-hand[257] but this may be indicative of a general loss of regard for clerics following the denunciations against earlier monks and friars. It would have been a brave individual to publicly support the Church of Rome during much of the later sixteenth century and the private thoughts of the population were naturally not recorded. Until the 1790s a manuscript survived which recounted the misfortunes of those Devonians who had converted ancient Catholic buildings: one family who used a font in their pound house allegedly suffered the extinction of their line while another in Broadclyst were doomed to disturbed nights after they used a chapel for a brew-house. Their beer was never fit to drink as well.[258] How widespread any such misgivings were in Devon can only be speculated upon.

The continued survival of so many Passion symbols on bench ends after the Reformation raises questions as to whether these carvings were considered appropriate for a Church of England building. There was considerable change, in both destruction and re-creation during one period of fourteen years. The first Reformation act against images came in 1547 with an injunction against images. This resulted in an onslaught on glass, shrines and statues. Three years later, in 1550,

wooden tables replaced stone altars but then Queen Mary reinstated them three years later only for her successor and sister Elizabeth to take them out and return the wooden tables. Another change took place two years later when the rood lofts of church screens were ordered to be destroyed but each church was meant to retain a partition between the nave and chancel.[259] There were no specific acts on seating but no doubt these other laws impacted upon the carvings on bench ends.

It is interesting to compare the Passion images with the aforementioned 50 carvings of saints. Only eleven of these are in south or east Devon: Combe-in-Teignhead has three benches with seven saints, Pinhoe near Exeter has a bench end with St Michael after whom it was dedicated and there are three others at Yarcombe on the border with Dorset. The vast majority of the carvings of saints are in the same part of Devon that has the symbols of the Passion.

Most of the saints' images are intact such as those at Combe-in-Teignhead. Fifteen others appear to have been defaced. All five at West Woolfardisworthy have been deliberately damaged or have wear and tear. There are two saints on one bench end at Sutcombe and their faces have clearly been shorn off. This is similar to the treatment at Braunton where six of the nine saints have also been defaced. One bench end is particularly interesting in that the saint on the left has deliberately had its face removed while that on the right

is unmarked. The collection at High Bickington, the highest in Devon with 22 saints, is also curious in this respect. Each saint retains his face but an additional figure of a praying monk, known locally as Athelstone, has either severe wear and tear or has been deliberately defaced. Bishops at Abbotsham and Braunton are also facially incomplete.

Nearly a century ago Reverend Chanter speculated that the carvings represent the continued allegiance of local people to Catholicism. He wrote of Braunton that 'Catholic feeling was very strong in this parish all through Elizabeth's reign – the holy relics of St Brannock were still displayed, vestments retained such as the chasuble and cope, also lights, incense, surpliced choir, guilds and brotherhood days'.[260] It is likely that popular attachment to Roman Catholicism began to diminish throughout Devon in the second half of the sixteenth century, a period that was dominated by the long conflict with Spain. Devon was the centre of privateering and it was a Devonian,

Above: High Bickington.
***Right:** A bench end at Braunton where one saint has been defaced.*

Sir Francis Drake, who led the national and local efforts. It was at this time that Adam Wyott, the town clerk of Barnstaple who was from Braunton, looked with admiration and envy on the rich prize ships that were being brought into North Devon. He does not appear to have approved of Puritanism but noted in his town chronicle that it was to the 'admiration of all protestants' that in 1586 there was a 'trental of sermons' at Pilton and Shirwell churches during which men and women attended 'an exercise or holy fast'.[261] Interestingly, neither of these churches have Passion carvings. It is only possible to speculate that by this date popular feeling identified English Protestantism with patriotism given the enemy was Roman Catholic. Even so, there must have been a degree of pragmatism in that the great profits being made in Devon's fishing trade were overwhelmingly dependent upon Roman Catholic markets in France, Portugal, Spain and Italy. Moreover, it was the continued practice of non-meat days prescribed by Rome that kept demand for English fish high.[262] A considerable number of the parishes with Passion carvings are those which would have sent men to the fisheries. After the Reformation

these men stopped naming their ships after saints but continued to earn a livelihood that was dependent upon Catholic customs.

The best known Elizabethan in this area with Passion carvings was Sir Richard Grenville *(left)* whose death, on the *Revenge* in 1591, took place after the carvings were made. Through his landholdings Grenville had considerable influence on both sides of the counties' border and his wife was from Monkleigh whose church has a collection of religious carvings. Kilkhampton, where the couple's mansion was located, also has a considerable number of Passion images.[263] Despite Grenville's reputation as an advocate for English nationalism, in its expansion and war against Spain, there is no evidence that he exerted any pressure in removing Passion carvings but he was able to live with them.

All parish clerics, and presumably the churchwardens, would have been familiar in 1547 with the order of the Privy Council that all 'popish and superstitious images' were to be destroyed. It is known that such items were removed from parish churches and either destroyed or secreted-away. The bonfire in Exeter's Cathedral Close in 1550s, in which religious objects were burned, must have been discussed throughout the diocese.[264] Perhaps because of this any benches with offending images were defaced or destroyed but no documents record this. The survival of the remaining Passion carvings may well indicate that they were not considered contradictory to Church of England doctrine. Saints were defaced but at least some Passion images were left. This has parallels with Devon's screens where the roods were destroyed and images of saints were defaced or painted over but many screens were left to stand intact. The bench ends' survival may be due to Passion images being illustrations of the sacrifice of Jesus and not being connected to any saint's cult.

It may also be relevant that these North Devon parishes and those in Cornwall were the most remote from the centre of the diocese at Exeter. It is here that the bishop would have been least able to fully extend reforming practices. The Passion images are also in lower-population areas where there was less wealth. Churches in the east and west were more likely to be able to afford new seats that would not have had Passion images. Equally, given that it is in these areas that plain Gothic tracery has survived, it may be that these carvings were never in the south and east of the diocese.

Finally, one of the most likely reasons for the distribution pattern may lie with the craftsmen themselves. It appears that the two high moorlands of Devon restricted the spread of carving styles. Exmoor and Dartmoor were effective barriers to the sharing of styles between parishes. It is noticeable that Dartmoor lies between the two areas where either plain Gothic arches or Passion symbols lie. Likewise, there are no

Crowcombe in Somerset.

159

similarities in the carving of West Somerset bench ends and those of north-east Devon where Exmoor lies. These parishes are in a cluster to the west of the river Parrett and Bridgwater. They are dominated by the workmanship of Simon Warman, a local man who was carving from the 1540s through to 1585.[265] His existing work is distinctive with a rigid use of foliage and, unlike other Somerset carvers, he favoured decorative borders. The bench ends are dissimilar from those in Devon and demonstrate either the influence of one man on local design or how collectively a style of ornamentation can be created and widely utilised. Gothic designs run along the southern parishes of Somerset and through to Wells with one parish, Stoke Sub Hamdon, having a distinctly different use of Gothic motifs from other churches.

The story of the crucifixion can still be told from the Passion images. The accepted narrative in the fifteenth century was that Judas betrayed Jesus for a bag of **thirty pieces of silver**. In the garden of Gethsemane at the Last Supper Jesus symbolised the sharing of his blood with wine (**cup**) and his body for bread (**plate**). Jesus was subsequently arrested and soldiers carried **lanterns** as it was night. Peter attacked one of the men, Malchus, with his **sword** and cut off his right **ear**. Peter subsequently denied knowing Jesus at dawn when a **cock** was crowing. Pontius Pilate, the Roman official in Jerusalem, washed his hands (**ewers**) after the trial and then Jesus was bound with **cords** at a **pillar** and **whips** scourged his skin. The

West Woolfardisworthy.

Abbotsham.

Broadwoodwidger.

Down St Mary.

Roman soldiers crowned him with **thorns**, provided him with a **sceptre of reed** and pierced his side with a **spear**. The soldiers mocked him in **spitting** and striking him with a **wooden staff**. Whilst carrying his cross Veronica wiped Christ's face with her **veil**. At the **cross** Jesus was

Lapford.

Sutcombe.

Northlew.

Broadwoodwidger.

Marwood.

Westleigh.

Monkleigh.

fixed with **nails hammered** to his **feet** and **hands**. He was offered a **reed** or **branch** of hyssop on which was a vinegar-laden **sponge** for Christ to drink. Whilst waiting for him to die Roman soldiers gamble with **dice** for ownership of Jesus' **robe**. After his death the **nails** were removed by **pincers**, a **ladder** was used to take down his body and his body was treated with **ointment** and wrapped in **linen**.

A number of images are highly ambiguous. The plate and ewer could indicate the Last Supper or Pilate

161

washing his hands of any guilt. A large vessel could depict an aspersorium (for Jesus blessing his disciples) or the ointment jar.[266] There is also an ambiguous image at Monkleigh of a man who has a substance erupting from his mouth: this might have been meant to depict one of the Roman soldiers who spat on Christ.[267] On a bench end at Abbotstham is IHS to the right and on the left is an inverted anchor which might indicate the loss of hope. Ashwater has on one shield a hand holding a cross while to its right is a shield with a hand holding what might be a palm or it could be the hyssop branch.

The images of the Passion were also elsewhere in churches. A few examples can still be found in glass, generally in the highest position in a window. For example, Sidmouth and Whitestone have the Five Wounds in ancient glass as does Doddiscombsleigh. A spectacular example relating to the Passion is the Seven Sacraments window also at Doddiscombsleigh. This fifteenth-century glass features Christ at the centre with the blood from his Five Wounds passing to the sacraments. There is not another like it in Devon and the bordering counties of Somerset has one at East Brent, Dorset has a partial one at Bradford Abbas and the Cornish church of St Kew has images of the Crucifixion.[268]

Left: *Monkleigh.*   **Right:** *Weare Giffard and Sidmouth.*

Less evidence can be discovered for images of the Passion in Devon's screens but there are a number of roof bosses with similar motifs. Victorian restorers used all three to reinstate symbols of the Passion and it can be difficult to ascertain which are ancient from those which have been relatively recently installed. There are three other good examples in Devon of images relating to the Passion. Ashton has a wall painting of the Mass of St Gregory which has many of these motifs, the Kirkham Chantry in Paignton has similar carved representations which are in remarkably good condition and there is a crucifixion scene on medieval tombs at Mortehoe and South Pool.

East Budleigh's carvings are of particular interest given that shortly after the benches were erected the Raleighs acquired a reputation for being keen Protestants. In 1549, when Exeter was besieged by the Prayer Book rebels, Walter Raleigh, father of Sir Walter Raleigh, was riding to Exeter when he passed an elderly woman in Clyst St Mary. He chastened her for having rosary beads and informed her of the penalties for continuing Roman Catholic practices. They departed on bad terms and she informed her neighbours, perhaps with some enlargement, that Raleigh had threatened the village if it did not conform with Protestant practice. Raleigh was then set upon by the villagers and forced to seek safety in a

Left: Doddiscombsleigh.
Right: *Detail of the glass at Whitestone.*

nearby chapel. Some mariners from Exmouth rescued him although he was subsequently recaptured outside Exeter and incarcerated in St Sidwell's Church.[269] The East Budleigh carvings have no religious elements except for angels holding heraldic shields. It is unlikely that Raleigh would have been sympathetic to his home church installing or retaining carvings that would have been in any way religiously controversial. The East Budleigh carvings are a mixture of Gothic foliate and Renaissance design but they also have a good mix of Village Art. In this respect they share qualities with Sandford and a limited number of other Devon parishes. In the mid-nineteenth century the Exeter Diocesan Architectural Society pronounced them 'strikingly good and pleasing'.[270] What is remarkable about them is how differently they were carved from those in North Devon.

165

Craftsmen: joiners and carpenters

The identities of the carvers remain frustratingly elusive. Only a few Pre-Reformation individuals were recorded. John Mayne was the carver at Ashburton in 1511 and Matthew More created the seats at Plympton St Mary twenty years earlier [271] but Hugh Prust of Hartland had seats made by an unnamed carver at Bideford in 1530.[272] No others have yet been found in Devon's early accounts.

Left: Sutcombe.
Below: Ottery St Mary.

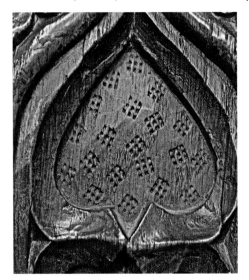

The ethnicity of Devon's late medieval and post-Reformation craftsmen has been debated for many years: Hoskins believed the men that created the screens were Devonians unlike others who thought they were Flemish. In the 1540s John Parrys of Northlew began carving Atherington's rood-loft. He travelled only some fifteen miles to work at Atherington if it was carved in situ. The carving was finished by Roger Down and John Hyll of the bordering parish of Chittlehampton. Winkleigh's screen was carved from about 1512 to 1515 by two men, John Clement and John Kellegh, but their places of residence are not recorded.[273] Down, Hill and Clement, of Landkey, were listed in their respective parishes in a separate tax list of 1524 but were not noted as being foreign.[274] Braunton's pews were erected by 1560 through to the 1630s and in one year, 1583, it was recorded that they had been brought from Barnstaple where presumably the seats had been carved. Several men created the seating, in either carving them or in their maintenance, and these included such individuals as Robert Acland, William Clifford, John Courtney, John Nicholl and the aptly named Richard

Wood.[275] There is no indication these were not local men. The evidence points to Devon craftsmen by the late 1500s. In the following century men such as Mark Baker, a carpenter of Sheldon, was erecting seats at nearby Dunkeswell. Devon's churchwardens' accounts provide no indication from the Elizabethan period onwards of foreign craftsmen being employed to work on seating.[276]

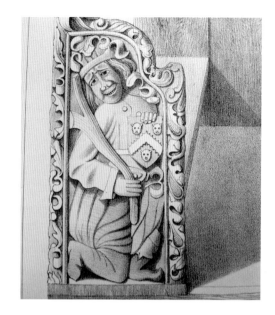

In 1908 it was Francis Bond who had debated whether Flemings, Spaniards or Bretons carved Devon's screens. There has been speculation over the screen at Colebrooke which Bond thought was the work of Breton workmen. Most recently John Allan has taken up the argument and has convincingly shown their activity in Devon in the early 1500s.[277] It is likely the current prayer desk in the church was the work of the same pre-Reformation Bretons. This, like the screen, is atypical for Devon.

There are few pre-Reformation churchwardens' accounts for Devon and thus it is difficult to determine if foreign craftsmen were building the benches. In the late 1520s Breton carvers erected additional seats at Bodmin but so far no evidence has turned up for similar work in Devon.[278] The Plymouth borough accounts do not record the identify of the early seat carvers but there are references to paying 'Pers the Frenchman' for nine and a half days' work putting up plaster in the guildhall and castle in 1502. Another workman, Nicholas Martyn, presumably a local man, was doing the same work.[279] Twenty-two years later, in 1524, John Pyers, a carpenter, was listed in a Plymouth tax list but he was not noted as being foreign.[280] It is likely that it will never be known who was responsible for the medieval bench ends given that the relevant documents have not survived. It may be telling that no foreign craftsmen have yet been identified although

Right: The ends to the prayer desk at Colebrooke.

168

Left: The wild men at Combe-in-Teignhead.

miles from Northlew, also employed a carpenter with the name John Paris. He was paid the high sum of thirteen pounds for unspecified work.[282] A workman with a similar name, John Peirs, erected seats at Hartland nearly one hundred years later.[283] It may be just another fluke that the parish accounts show an earlier payment, in 1526, for carpentry to one John Hill but he is likely to have been the aforementioned carpenter of Chittlehampton.[284]

The carvers named in the Post-Reformation accounts all appear to be English. In 1556 William Maser erected seats at Tavistock and in 1573 Plymouth Corporation paid one Vincent Scoble £4 5s 10d for 'the making of five pews' in St Andrew's Church.[285] Braunton's named carvers also appear to be English and others were not identified, in 1579, 1583 and 1593, but recorded only as joiners. One entry, for 1583, noted the 'joiner and his company' were paid

Northlew's Parrys, for one, was not foreign but he may well have had French ancestry.[281] It may also just be a coincidence but in 1529 the parish of Chagford, only 15

for setting up the seats. Presumably this was similar to other parishes in that, like today, the joiner did not work alone.[286] In 1612 Joel Hammond built seats at Winkleigh and in the early 1660s Edward Pike, a joiner of Exeter,

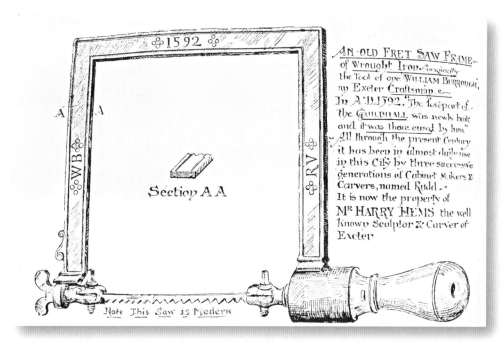

Left: *Elizabethan saw which worked wood at Exeter Guildhall.*

made them at St Stephen's Church in Exeter. By that late date it is unlikely he was carving bench ends but high pews.[287]

While Devon, unlike our neighbouring counties of Somerset and Cornwall, does not have an ancient bench end signed by a maker, it does have another means to help identify individuals. The benches themselves provide clues that have hitherto escaped attention. The craftsmen occasionally embellished their work with secondary decoration after the carving was completed.

This work can be categorised in three main ways.

Gouges were the least accomplished of all the marks and were used to bring out elementary design. The effect is slightly erratic with differences between the marks. Much more uniform were punch marks.[288] These are the most visible of the three forms. Punches were made by a hand-held tool at the end of which was a metal design that could be thumped into the wood. The effect was to provide the same constant shape. There are nearly 50 different punch marks to be found across Devon and a quarter of churches with ancient bench ends have punches or one of the other marks. Some churches, such as East Budleigh, employed a number of punch marks while others only had one.

One of the most common punch designs is of a simple circle. Some have an inner point within that

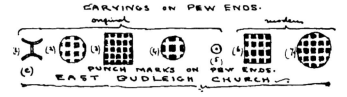

The East Budleigh punch marks.

170

Left: The missing bench end at East Budleigh.

circle. The other most commonly-found punch mark is that of a regularised set of points set either within a square or circle. The majority of the punch marks are one of these two types. There are others that are markedly different. Shillingford has a cross, Lewtrenchard and Parracombe St Petrock[289] have designs reminiscent of the sun and Sandford has two unusual ones with the most remarkable being similar to a clover. The small collection of ends at Powderham Castle Chapel share three punch marks and one of them looks like a circular Union Jack.

The punches were presumably individually created for workmen but it is debatable whether they lasted beyond a lifetime or were handed down from one generation to another. It is also interesting to speculate if the craftsmen created the pattern with the intended seat designs in mind. It is difficult to gauge whether a particular punch mark was used on bench ends in two churches but this might be the case with one seat at Abbotsham and the bench ends at nearby Monkleigh. There are also similarities between a punch mark at East Budleigh, Ottery St Mary and Venn Ottery. The use of punches can show that in a number of these churches that these tools were employed in entire collections of seats. The benches at Lewtrenchard, for example, are dominated by the use of a single tool. Punch marks also help identify the origins of bench ends. One such seat was photographed nearly a century ago but has since

Lifton.

Parracombe.

Sandford.

Powderham Castle Chapel.

Broadwoodwidger.

Lewtrenchard.

Puddington.

disappeared from its church: the punch mark is one that was used in East Budleigh and helps confirm that is where the bench had been erected.[290]

The use of the punch varies stylistically. There is an exceptional use at Lewtrenchard where the carver not only used his 'sun' punch to highlight areas but he also filled the background with it. St Michael's upper body has them in delicate lines but he also decorated the dragon and the souls he is weighing as well as the scales. The carver carried this through to his other benches as well. The mark demonstrates the use of a single tool, and perhaps of one individual, in making these seats. Puddington has only a handful of ancient bench ends: each employs a different Gothic diaper pattern, but the carver used his eight-point 'wheel' punch mark to great effect. This use gives them a highly distinctive character.

East Budleigh's carvers employed six different punch marks. Some bench ends have a variety of patterns and they form an integral part of the overall design. The

Marwood has a use of punch marks which is all but unique to itself.

seat dated 1537, that of the Raleigh family, has a more restrained use of punches and deployed only two patterns. Huntsham's dated seat, of 1534, has a similar punch mark to those at East Budleigh. The East Budleigh benches have both Renaissance and Gothic designs and the punches are used throughout particularly in an inner frame to the border. Similar designs are to be found at Sandford but here the use of punch marks is muted although distinguished by the use of three variations of a design unique to it. The 'Sandford clover' punch mark is almost entirely restricted to serve as background embellishment for flowing foliate designs. Two other smaller clover designs are also used. One of them is incised.

Marwood has a use of punch marks which is all but unique to itself. The craftsman embellished his shields with initials but the carving is rivalled in its design by the use of punch marks. These are as prominent as the carving and are supplemented by stipples, the single mark made by the point of a simple metal instrument. This mix of punches and stipples has

Northleigh.

resulted in a striking design which is instantaneously
recognisable as being Marwood. Neighbouring churches
which have bench ends, such as Ashford, and Mortehoe,
have no such decoration. At Marwood the stipples and
punches are used in rustic if not meandering lines and
occasionally in what looks like a haphazard fashion. It has
this in common with the carver at Braunton who either
left work unfinished or had as his design a sporadic use
of punch marks in some cusps and foils but not within
others which were on the same bench end.

Stippling is used to great effect in the foliage design
in several churches such as West Worlington where it is
used en masse and also to produce delicate and simple
lines. At Northleigh stipples pick out the centres and

Churston Ferrers.

176

Braunton.

petals of flowers in a similar way to nearby Whimple. However, Northleigh has distinctive six to nine petalled daisy-like flowers which are positioned at the top of great long stems. Stoke Canon also lightly picks out its flowers with stippling but in neighbouring Rewe the stipples also follow the setting-out lines of the carver's initial plans for the bench end.

Scoring, in which the wood is superficially cut rather than as deeply as in normal carving, is used in a number of different churches. The most practical use is probably at Hartland where several bench ends have names lightly incised in the wood. There is also a pair of ends in which the main design, a Renaissance figure

which nearly fills the panel, has been lightly scored. Other churches also have examples of scoring used to better achieve the intended design. At Newton St Petrock and St Giles on the Heath there are some simple but effective lines that supplement the main motifs with graceful flourishes. At Dowland paint was applied within deeper scoring on two ends. One bench is dated 1546. The top of the linen-fold bench end at Ottery St Mary is picked out with stippling but one end has an elaborate shape scored in one fold. The design is created partly by carving but the butterfly shape is mostly achieved by graceful scoring. Linenfold often has delicate lines carved at the top or base of the folds and examples can be found in other panels at Yarcombe.[291]

Mortehoe has one bench end with Gothic arches filled with shields with initials. Above and below the shields are designs, somewhat like the sun, which were lightly etched into the wood.

Marks were also applied to the borders. At Shillingford a punch mark runs along the foliate border and outside of the tracery design. There is also stippling within the border at Northleigh and East Budleigh amongst other places.

Two churches have evidence of the tools these craftsmen used. Abbotsham has a bench end with two shields of carpenter's tools while Bridford has another shield with ones which are more specialised. In its chancel is a seat which is reputed to have been

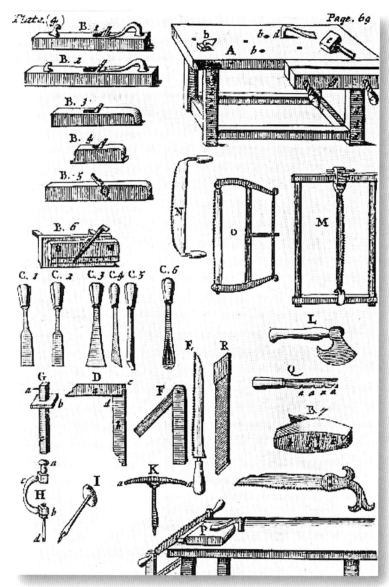

Carpentry tools, 1703, with C1-6 scalpels.

constructed in the early nineteenth century. The rector, Reverend William Carrington, recorded that he used old bench ends to create pews for his family and took apart 'an old carved oak chest'. He used other pieces to make up a chair. Carrington retained two poppy heads of 'figures in monkish habits' (now difficult to identify as they have lost their heads) and employed parts of the chest for the back and central part. On the sides he used two ancient bench ends.

The chair has on one side blank Gothic tracery while the other has heraldic arms which Carrington noted. In the top left are the arms of the Champernowne family, on the top right a defaced lion, on the bottom right a drawing compass, and finally, in the bottom left hand corner, a rack of four joiners' scalpels. Each of the latter have different ends.[292] No other church has such carving although Bickleigh near Tiverton has a bench end with a figure holding a bag of tools, possibly for wood-carving.

There are also marks, presumably by joiners, left behind on the benches. One can be seen in a bench at Broadwoodwidger. This six-pointed daisy wheel has in all probability been achieved with the use of a compass. To its right is a circle, possibly an incomplete design. Hartland has a similar design on one bench and a more complicated one on another.[293] These have been interpreted as ritual protection marks[294] but their purpose within or on the outside of benches remains uncertain.

There are others in Devon churches, such as on the column at Parracombe St Petrock, on the medieval stone screen at Colyton and in the roof space of Bradworthy Church,[295] but what purpose these served can only be conjectured. They do not form part of the overall design and are a mild form of defacement.

The subtlety of this secondary carving can be easily seen on Devon's as yet earliest dated bench-end, that thought to be from Lifton and now

Left: A 'protection mark' at Broadwoodwidger.

housed at Launceston Museum. This panel, of 1489, is divided into two parts both of which are filled with foliage. The top section has, at the top, the coat of arms of Patrick Holiburton, rector of Lifton, with the text on the left 'mercies of the Lord in eternal...'[296] Both sections have short swirling lines which are filled with stipple marks. They provide a decorative background which is not immediately apparent. Another of Devon's earliest dated series of benches, those at Coldridge, has particularly light and elegant secondary carving along the border and in the main panel.

All of these secondary design elements provide an additional layer of interest in Devon's ancient bench ends and demonstrate a considered quality in the approach to the overall designs.

Conclusion

Benches have been a feature of Devon's churches for nearly six hundred years. In that time they have been carved, fallen out of fashion, seen a Renaissance and now face, in some churches, an uncertain future. Bench ends have not received the consideration that they deserve. The beauty of their craftsmanship has gone largely unnoticed despite there being local distinctiveness to the carvings. South Devon has favoured plain Gothic tracery while North Devon has specialised in adding shields and sometimes embellishing them with religious motifs. The Village Art is another type of carving, expressive of the villagers for whom they were made. Renaissance imagery runs throughout the county and was seldom a form separate from Gothic styles.

It is a myth that medieval churches did not have seating and it is often used as a justification for removing them today. Devon's earliest churchwardens' accounts show seats had been installed a century before the start of the Reformation. Benches were the favoured form of seat in the great church rebuilding of the fifteenth and early sixteenth centuries and their rich carvings are unique examples of local and in some instances, foreign, artistry. The Victorian appreciation of medieval carving as well as their perception of benches as an expression of Christian equality within a sacred space has bequeathed an outstanding historical legacy. The case for reappraising these centuries of craftsmanship is compelling.

Few individual seats can be firmly dated despite Devon having one of the greatest collections of documents in Britain. The new field of dendrology, the dating of wood through scientific analysis, may provide answers in the near future and help us to understand the complicated history of church seating in Devon. The continued survival of these rare and wonderful carvings depends upon a careful appreciation of the importance of this extraordinary legacy which has not only a local but a national significance.

Left: Four scalpels at Bridford.

Alwington.

Footnotes

1   All transfer dates taken from Hugh Peskett (ed.), *Guide to the Parish and Non-Parochial Registers of Devon and Cornwall, 1538 – 1837* (Devon & Cornwall Record Society, ES II, 1979).

2   Philip Nicholls, *Sir Francis Drake Revived* (1626).

3   John Brooking Rowe (ed), '*The Two Widecombe Tracts, 1638, giving a Contemporary Account of the great Storm, reprinted with an introduction*', Devon & Cornwall Notes & Queries, Vol. 3, 1905, appendix, 5-8.

4   Kate Clarke, 'Carved Bench Ends in Devon', *Transactions of the Exeter Diocesan Architectural Society, Third Series*, 3 (1920); E. A. K. Prideaux, 'Sutcombe Church and its Builders', *Devon & Cornwall Notes & Queries*, Vol. 8, 1915, appendix; Beatrix Cresswell, 'Sittings in Churches', *Devon & Cornwall Notes & Queries*, Vol. 9, Part 4, October 1916, 116-119.

5   J. Charles Cox, *Bench ends in English Churches* (Oxford, 1916), pages 74 to 90 cover Devon as well as F. E. Howard & F. H. Crossley, *English Church Woodwork* (1917) which has a section on benches and pews.

6   J. C. D. Smith, *Church Woodcarvings, a West Country Study* (Newton Abbot, 1969); J. M Slader, *The Churches of Devon* (Newton Abbot, 1968). See also J. C. D. Smith, '*The Bench ends of Devon*', *Devon Life*, Volume One, No. 6, July 1965, 34-5.

7   Stephen J. Hobbs, *St Nectan's: the question of a seat* (Hartland, 2005). There has also recently been the Sandford Heritage Group's Bench End Project which is the first parish-based group study of bench ends.

8   Francis Kelly, 'Post-Reformation church seating arrangements and bench assembly notation in two North Devon churches', 149-70 and Jo Cox, 'Some seating designs in churches by John Hayward of Exeter', 267-76, in Trevor Cooper and Sarah Brown (eds), *Pews, Benches and Chairs* (2011). See also Jo Cox, 'The Rise and the Fall of the Box Pew' and Joanna Mattingly, 'The origins of Devon Bench Ends', *Devon Buildings Group Newsletter*, Number 25, Summer 2007, 26-44, 8-11.

9   Nine of Exeter's ancient churches have not survived and most recently Creacombe and Monkton have been sold. There were 475 parishes in Devon that kept parishes registers at the time of the Reformation. A fuller note of some of the definitions that have been used for this study can be found with the Note & Acknowledgments. Every ancient church in Devon has been visited to search for bench ends but it is possible that some have been misidentified. For a thorough guide to the identification of these benches see Jerry Sampson, 'Medieval benches and bench ends of Somerset: towards an archaeological approach' in Trevor Cooper and Sarah Brown (eds), *Pews Benches and Chairs* (2011), 87-110.

10 Personal communication with Hugh Harrison; T. R. Owen, *St Brannock's Church, Braunton* (Braunton, 2010), 3; A bench made in 1496 at Plymouth Guildhall was also oak: Plymouth & West Devon Record Office, W130, folio 33.

11 John Wallis, *The Bodmin Register* (Bodmin, 1830), 33-5; Richard Ballard, *The Priory Church of St Andrew*, Stogursey (Stogursey, 1992), 46. Welsh wood came via Bridgwater for the rood loft for the church at Trull in the 1530s: McDermott, 'Early Bench ends', 120.

12 North Devon Record Office, 1677A/PW1A.

13 Devon Record Office, DD61409.

14 Devon Record Office, Chanter 864/360-2.

15 Most recently see Joanna Mattingley, 'The origins of Devon bench ends – the view from Cornwall', *Devon Buildings Group Newsletter*, Number 25, Summer 2007, 8; P. S. Barnwell, 'Seating in the nave of the pre-Reformation parish church', in Cooper and Brown, *Pews, Benches and Chairs*, 71.

16 Devon Record Office, Chanter 864. This was in St Tudy near Bodmin.

17 Devon Record Office, CC89/202.

18 Devon Record Office, 2935A-99/PW1/3.

19 See Devon Record Office, Principal Registry, Basket A, letters relating to seats, numbers 1600 to 1828, which notes some of the disputes mostly of the late seventeenth and eighteenth centuries.

20 Devon Record Office, 347A/99/PW2, page 7 & 3009A/99/PW1, pages 18 & 74.

21 J. Erskine Binney (ed.), *The Accounts of the Wardens of the Parish of Morebath, 1520-1573* (Exeter, 1904), 60.

22 Devon Record Office, Principal Registry, Basket A/1691; CC181/25.

23 Devon Record Office, Diocesan Faculty Causes, Blackawton, 1753 & 1762, Cadeleigh, 1766 and Broadwoodkelly, 1825.

24 Richard Polwhele, *The History of Devonshire* (1796), Vol. 3, 77.

25 Devon Record Office, Z19/21/6, pages 198-9.

26 Devon Record Office, Diocesan Faculty Causes, Chivelstone.

27 Devon Record Office, Principal Registry, Basket A/1669.

28 Devon Record Office, Principal Registry, Basket A/1634.

29 Devon Record Office, Principal Registry, 517/97.

30 Bridget Cherry and Nikolaus Pevsner, *Devon* (1989), 302; Devon Record Office, Diocesan Faculty Causes, Cruwys Morchard; Jo Cox, 'The Rise and Fall of the Box Pew', *Devon Buildings Group Newsletter Number 25*, Summer 2007, 32.

31 Plymouth & West Devon Record Office, 1511/2.

32 *Exeter Flying Post*, 19 November 1812.

33 J. Medley, 'The advantages of open seats', *Transactions of the Exeter Diocesan Architectural Society* (1843), I, 157.

34 George Oliver and John Pike Jones, *The Ecclesiastical Antiquities of Devon and Cornwall* (Exeter, 1828).

35 *Exeter Flying Post*, 18 June 1884; *Western Times*, 17 June 1884.

36 Beatrix F. Cresswell, 'Sittings in Church', *Devon & Cornwall Notes & Queries*, Volume 9, Part 4, October 1916, 119. William Spreat also noted this at Chittlehampton: William Spreat, *Picturesque Sketches of the Churches of Devon* (Exeter, 1842), description for plates 25 to 27.

37 See Devon Record Office, CC89/6, for the testimony of Christopher Hillarson who had refused to pay the yearly fee of four shillings and four pence of what he described as the 'seidge or seat money'. For another use see Devon Record Office, Chanter 733/9-11, Black Torrington, plan.

38 Stanhope Nourse, 'Butts and Tutts', *Devon & Cornwall Notes & Queries*, Volume 7, Part 1, January 1912, 41-2. Clawton also had tits: R. Pearse Chope, 'Clawton Wardens' Accounts', *Devon & Cornwall Notes & Queries*, Volume 13, Part 6, 1925, 258. Butts, tuts and lofts are defined as such in the Oxford English Dictionary. R. Pearse Chope, *Hartland Glossary*, for 1637 'toyte' while for 1647 'tit'.

39 I am grateful to Janet Henwood for the following extract from the East Stonehouse Chapel vestry minutes on the duties of the butt-woman in 1839. Interestingly, it does not mentioned butts: *'To dust and clean the church including the lower windows on the inside, to attend at all the three services on Sunday and at all other times when Divine Service is performed, also at all Marriages, Baptisms and Burials, to conduct herself with becoming decorum to the Minister, Chapel Wardens and all other persons having duty at the chapel, that she receive the sum of thirty shillings from the lighting fund hitherto paid for the evening service with the further sum of one pound one shilling for which she is to wash out the church once every year under the directions of the chapel wardens.'*

40 Mike Brown (ed.), *Buckland in the Moor Churchwarden Accounts 1632-91* (Dartmoor, 1995), no page number; Personal communication with Steve Hobbs.

41 Axminster, Bere Ferrers, Bigbury, Blackawton, Black Torrington, Bradford, Branscombe, Broadclyst, Broadhempston, Buckfastleigh, Crediton, Harberton, High Bickington, Loddiswell, Lustleigh, Marystow, Newton Ferrers, Ottery St Mary, Plympton St Mary, Pyworthy, Rewe, Sheepwash, South Brent and West Ogwell.

42 Robert Whiting, *The Blind Devotion of the People* (Cambridge, 1991), 193.

43 Pevsner, *Devon*, 636.

44 Marion Glasscoe, 'The Medieval Woodwork', 117-122, in Michael Swanton (ed.), *Exeter Cathedral – A Celebration* (Exeter, 1991).

45 Westcountry Studies Library, sx726.5/WES/EXE.

46 Devon Record Office, DD61038 & DD61203.

47 Devon Record Office, Chanter 864.

48 North Devon Record Office, 1677A/PW1A, an entry for 1581 notes 2 forms were with Thomas Nicholl, 1 in the chancel, 1 in the 'loft' by the organ, 1 in the chapel, 1 in the church house and 2 in the lime house.

49 Devon Record Office, Chanter 8540.

50 Devon Record Office, 2935A-99/PW1, 95 & 4344A-99/PW1, 216. In 1561 Crediton had its forms in the choir mended and in 1590 a substantial number of forms were built for the church: 2935A-99/PW1, 58, 304.

51 Cox, *Bench ends*, 4-6.

52 These are at Abbotsham, Alwington, Ashcombe, Ashford, Ashton, Ashwater, Atherington, Bere Ferrers, Bickleigh (nr Tiverton), Bideford, Bondleigh, Braunton, Bridford, Bridgerule, Broadhempston, Broadwoodwidger, Buckland Filleigh, Buckland Monachorum, Cadbury, Cheldon, Cheriton Bishop, Christow, Chudleigh, Churchstanton, Churston Ferrers, Clayhanger, Clovelly, Cockington, Coldridge, Colebrooke, Combe Martin, Combe-in-Teignhead, Cookbury, Countisbury, Crediton, Dartington, Doddiscombsleigh, Dolton, Dowland, Down St Mary, Drewsteignton, Dunchideock, East Budleigh, East Ogwell, Feniton, Frithelstock, George Nympton, Hartland, Hatherleigh, High Bickington, Honeychurch, Horwood, Huntsham, Ilsington, Inwardleigh, Kenn, Kenton, Kingsbridge, Kingston, Landcross, Lapford, Lewtrenchard, Lifton, Littleham (nr Bideford), Marwood, Modbury, Monkleigh, Mortehoe, Newton St Petrock, North Bovey, North Tawton, Northleigh, Northlew, Nymet Rowland, Ottery St Mary, Pancrasweek, Parracombe, Payhembury, Pinhoe, Plympton St Mary, Plymtree, Powderham, Puddington, Rewe, Roborough, Sandford, Satterleigh, Seaton, Shillingford, South Tawton, St Giles in the Heath, Shobrooke, Stockleigh Pomeroy, Stoke Canon, Stoke Gabriel, Stoke Rivers, Sutcombe, Swimbridge, Talaton, Tavistock, Tawstock, Tedburn St Mary, Tetcott, Thornbury, Thorverton, Throwleigh, Torbryan, Upton Hellions, Venn Ottery, Warkleigh, Weare Giffard, Welcombe, West Anstey, West Putford, West Woolfardisworthy, West Worlington, Westleigh, Whimple, Woodbury, Yarcombe. In addition to these churches, the Royal Albert Memorial Museum holds 8 bench ends for the churches of Clyst St George, Bere Ferrers and Staverton; The Victoria and Albert Museum also has a small collection of bench ends from the West Country. Powderham Castle Chapel also has a small collection of bench ends which are thought to have come from South Huish Church in 1867. Sampford Spiney and East Allington have reused later woodwork.

53 Hugh R. Watkin, *Dartmouth Vol. 1 Pre-Reformation* (Devonshire Association Parochial Histories No. 5, 1935), 305-6, 327, 335.

54 George Oliver and John Pike Jones, *Ecclesiastical Antiquities*, 34.

55 Frederick Bligh Bond, 'Devonshire Screens and Rood Lofts', *Transactions of the Devonshire Association*, Vol. 34, 1902, 534.

56 John Wallis, *The Bodmin Register* (Bodmin, 1830), 33-5.

57 Alison Hanham (ed.), *Churchwardens' Accounts of Ashburton*, 1479-1580 (Devon & Cornwall Record Society, NS Vol. 15, 1970), 5, 41, 44, 50, 52, 70, 63, 73, 162, 174, 182, 185, 187.

58 Seats were mended in 1527, 1530, 1536, 1542, 1564 and 1590. In 1538

trestles and seats were purchased but these may have been for the church-house. In 1573 seats were made for the church: Osborne, *Chagford Churchwarden Accounts*, 83, 104, 159, 202, 250, 142, 223.

59   Whiting, *Blind Devotion*, 241.

60   Plymouth & West Devon Record Office, W130, folios 27, 42, 84, 114 as seen in 2272, transcription by A. Norman; Robert Tittler, 'Seats of honour, seats of power: the symbolism of public seating in the English Urban Community, c.1560-1620', *Albion*, Vol. 24, No. 2, Summer 1992, 205-223.

61   Joanna Mattingley, 'The Origins of Devon bench ends – the view from Cornwall', *Devon Buildings Group Newsletter Number 25* (Summer, 2007), 8.

62   Marion Glasscoe and Michael Swanton, *Medieval Woodwork in Exeter Cathedral* (Exeter, 1978), 8-9. The cathedral's records show there were benches erected in 1330 and again in 1350: Audrey Erskine (ed.), *The accounts of the fabric of Exeter Cathedral, 1279-1353* (Devon & Cornwall Record Society, NS 24, 1981), II, 235, 286

63   Cox notes this as Monkleigh but this is probably a mistake for Landcross: Cox, *Bench Ends*, 86.

64   North Devon Record Office, 1677A/PW6.

65   North Devon Record Office, 1677A/PW1A; J. F. Chanter, T*he Church of St Brannock, Braunton* (Braunton, 1909), 8; T. R. Owen, *St Brannock's Church, Braunton* (Braunton, no date given but by 2006), 17-18.

66   Devon Record Office, CC3/139.

67   Devon Record Office, Dartmouth Corporation accounts.

68   For example, see Joanna Mattingly, 'The Dating of Bench ends in Cornish Churches', *Journal of the Royal Institution of Cornwall*, NS II, Vol. 1, Part 1, 1991, 58.

69   P. S. Barnwell, 'Seating in the nave of the pre-Reformation parish church', in Trevor Cooper and Sarah Brown, *Pews, Benches and Chairs* (2011), 82.

70   North Devon Record Office, 2288A/PF/3/6; Devon Record Office, 2954Aadd2/PF1; Devon Record Office, 3083/PF/1; North Devon Record Office, 2989A/PW6.

71   One example of this is Dartington: Devon Record Office, 347A-99/PW2.

72   I am grateful to John Allan for drawing this example to my attention.

73   Devon Record Office, 4344A-99/PW1, 211

74   Devon Record Office, 2935-99/PW1, 220.

75   Devon Record Office, 2935-99/PW1, 221. Hill was named as Richard Hill in 1584: 2935-99/PW1/263-4.

76   Devon Record Office, DD61351.

77   'for timber to make the frames of the pews between St George's Aisle & the font 4s 8d; for 2 fir boards for the same pews 4s; more paid for 2 fir boards to make forms for the same pews 20d; for 2 beech boards afore to line at for the same pews 10d; for hatch nails, board nails and sealing nails 20d; for jimmies & nails for the same pews 3s 4d;

for making of the same pews at 2s 4d a pew 11s 8d… for a fir board to make the seats under the pulpit 2s; for 2 transoms for the same seats 12d; for fir boards for the same seats & other boards and half a cushion 16d; for a pound spikes & 8 pennyworth of nails 11d; for 4 pair of jimmies for the doors for the same seats 12d; for 2 carpenters to make the same seats 5s… for the mending of Joan Davis' pew and Wotton's wife's pew and for the jimmies, boards & nails for the same 10d… for a board to sit upon that goeth along under the pulpit 8d; to the carpenters to set the same board along by the seats 2d; for a fir board to help make the 3 new seats by the south side of the church 20d; for a transom & another fir board to make studdles for the same seats 2s; for 3 pairs jimmies & for mending of 3 old jimmies & for nails to set the same 12d; for other nails as board nails, hatch nails for the same pews & about the church as doth appear 8d; to a carpenter for making of the same pews 3s… for a transom to make morts of the pews & a plank & for 3 fir boards for the same pews 5s; for 5 other pieces timber to make muntins & 3 fir boards 6s 10d; for jimmies, nails & board nails, hatch nails for the same pews 5s 2d; for 3 pounds of iron *clamis & spikes* 9d; for setting of the 2 planks by Saint George Aisle 4d; for making of the pews by the north doors 11s 8d; to workmen at Mr Mayor's commandment 12d… for 3 fir boards & ½ a board & a plank 5s; for making of the long seat & 2 other seats in the tower and for mending of the seats behind the church door & for the legs under the benches from the font to the chapel [no sum provided]…': Devon Record Office, DD61409.

78   Westcountry Studies Library, s726.5/DEV/DAV U, Church Notes [in the] East of Devon, 139.

79   The listed building survey recorded East Allington as having a bench end with the date 1633 but the panel is the wrong shape for the end of a bench. It could possibly be part of a high pew but may have been made for the screen. Dartmouth St Saviours has a wood fragment with the date 1630 which is now part of a reader's desk.

80   Talland and Lanteglos-by-Fowey have interesting seventeenth-century transitional seats.

81   Another Devon example is Shobrooke which has some seventeenth-century carving.

82   Alan Endacott, *All Saints' Parish Church & St James' Chapel, Okehampton; A History & Tour* (Okehampton, 2006), 19-20.

83   Devon Record Office, Principal Registry, 517/177.

84   Devon Record Office, Chanter 861/395-404.

85   Devon Record Office, Diocesan Faculty Causes, Clyst Hydon.

86   Devon Record Office, 608Aadd3/PF3.

87   These are the years for which they were given permission: Chanter 67/112, 162, 257.

88   Devon Record Office, Principal Registry, 517/191-2.

89   Devon Record Office, Principal Registry, 517/168.

90   Devon Record Office, Principal Registry, 517/147.

91 Devon Record Office, Principal Registry, Basket A, 1605.

92 Devon Record Office, Principal Registry, 517/136.

93 Devon Record Office, Principal Registry, Basket A, 1795.

94 Devon Record Office, Diocesan Faculty Causes, Cornwood, 1699.

95 Devon Record Office, Principal Registry, Basket A, Clayhidon, 1805.

96 Devon Record Office, Diocesan Faculty Petitions, Cadbury, 1744.

97 Devon Record Office, Chanter 859/166-7.

98 Devon Record Office, Diocesan Faculty Causes, Cadeleigh, 1766, Colebrooke, 1763.

99 North Devon Record Office, 834A/PW1.

100 Devon Record Office, Principal Registry, Basket A/1799.

101 In 1836 curtains at East Budleigh were complained about because they had been erected without permission: Devon Record Office, Principal Registry, Basket A, 1610.

102 Devon Record Office, 2610M-O/F3, there are no page numbers.

103 F. C. Hingeston-Randolph, *Records of a rocky shore* (1876), 24.

104 W. P. S. 'Nooks and Corners of Devon', *Exeter Flying Post*, 20 July 1848.

105 F. C. Hingeston-Randolph, *Records of a rocky shore* (1876), 20.

106 F. C. Hingeston-Randolph, *Records of a rocky shore* (1876), 22.

107 R. C. R., 'Account of the tiles, seats &c at Down St Mary, Devon', *Gentleman's Magazine*, 1822, part ii, page 209.

108 George Oliver and John Pike Jones, *Ecclesiastical Antiquities*, x.

109 Plymouth & West Devon Record Office, 723, page 9.

110 T. G. Holt, 'George Oliver, Antiquary, from his letters', *Transactions of the Devonshire Association*, Vol. 119, 1987, 53-65; T. Cann Hughes, 'Rev. John Pike Jones', *Devon & Cornwall Notes & Queries*, Volume 3, Part 1, 1906, 193-5.

111 George Oliver and John Pike Jones, *Ecclesiastical Antiquities*, 24.

112 Westcountry Studies Library, sxB/HAT/0001/540, page 405.

113 Cox, Bench ends, 74; J. Medley, 'The advantages of open seats', *Transactions of the Exeter Diocesan Architectural Society* (1843), I, 157.

114 The Victorians also brought chairs into their churches: Trevor Cooper (ed.), 'Movable benches or chairs? Correspondence in *The Ecclesiologist 1854-6*', Trevor Cooper and Sarah Brown (eds), *Pews, Benches and Chairs* (2011), 237-56.

115 Westcountry Studies Library, Rough Notes, sx726.5/WES/EXE.

116 *Exeter Flying Post*, 3 July 1889; *Western Times*, 5 July 1889.

117 *Exeter Flying Post*, 16 June 1875; *Western Times*, 11 June 1875.

118 *Exeter Flying Post*, 9 July 1862.

119 *Exeter Flying Post*, 7 June 1855, 28 July 1880; *Woolmers Exeter Gazette*, 9 June 1855; *Western Times*, 27 July 1880.

120 *Exeter Flying Post*, 13 February 1867.

121 *Exeter Flying Post*, 1 November 1865; *Western Times*, 31 October 1865.

122 *Exeter Flying Post*, 7 November 1883; *Western Times*, 2 November 1883.

123 Devon Record Office, Chanter 70/42; North Devon Record Office, 7621A/PW4.

124 North Devon Record Office, 3834A/PW1. *The North Devon Journal* reported 'all the ends of the open seats which are restored on their modet there was some notable carving representing a history of the betrayal and death of the saviour. What of the old can be preserved is replaced, and the others are carved *facsimile* of their predecessors. Mr Mathew Isaccs of Barnstaple is executing this part of the restoration under the immediate direction of the vicar.

125 Westcountry Studies Library, S726.5/DEV/DAV U, Church Notes [in the] North of Devon, 53.

126 *Exeter Flying Post*, 30 November 1854 & 19 June 1856; *Woolmer's Exeter Gazette*, 14 June 1856.

127 They included G. E. Paterson, E. A. Tanqueray and E. A. Green from 1902 to 1928.

128 *Exeter Flying Post*, 22 July 1885.

129 *Western Daily Mercury*, 23 October 1874; John B. Woollocombe, *From Morn til Eve* (1898).

130 *The British Architect*, 19 October 1883.

131 *The Illustrated Carpenter and Builder*, 1 January 1886.

132 The biographical details of Hems are taken from his scrapbooks housed at the Westcountry Studies Library.

133 Devon Record Office, Diocesan Faculty Petitions, Lydford 14 & 15.

134 *St Peter's Church, Stoke Fleming* (Stoke Fleming, no date given), 4.

135 *Violet Pinwill a Devon artist; a memoir compiled by members of her family* (no date or place of publication given).

136 'The Alwington Bible'; a guide to the pew ends in St Andrew's Church, Alwington* (Alwington, no date given); *The Builder*, 25 January 1879.

137 Devon Record Office, CC4A/86 & Principal Registry, 517/Clawton.

138 Devon Record Office, Diocesan Faculty Causes, Wembury, 1663.

139 Devon Record Office, CC89/6.

140 Devon Record Office, CC3/138.

141 Devon Record Office, CC89/154.

142 Robert Cornish (ed.), *Kilmington Church Wardens' Accounts* (Exeter, 1901), 99.

143 North Devon Record Office, 1843A/PW1.

144 North Devon Record Office, 1201A/PW1.

145 Devon Record Office, Chanter 8540.

146 Ivon L. Gregory (ed.), *Hartland Church Accounts, 1597-1706* (Frome, 1950), 142.

147 Devon Record Office, Diocesan Faculty Causes, Plymouth, 25 August 1646.

148 Devon Record Office, Diocesan Faculty Causes, Tiverton.

149 Devon Record Office, C3/137, CC4A/52 & Dartmouth Corporation Records, Fifteenth and Sixteenth Century Church Accounts; J. Brooking Rowe, *A history of the borough of Plympton Erle* (Exeter, 1906), 236-7.

150 Devon Record Office, CC4A/52.

151 Devon Record Office, Chanter 71/200.

152 Devon Record Office, Principal Registry, Basket A/1827.

153 Devon Record Office, Diocesan Faculty Causes, Cruwys Morchard, 1701.

154 Devon Record Office, CC181, Littleham.

155 Devon Record Office, Diocesan Faculty Causes, Atherington.

156 Devon Record Office, Principal Registry, 517/203 (Stoke Damerel).

157 Katherine L. French, 'The seat under Our Lady: Gender and Seating in Late Medieval English Parish Churches', in Virginia Chieffo Raguin and Sarah Stanbury, *Women's Space; patronage, place and gender in the Medieval Church* (Albany, 2005), 142-3.

158 Ethel Lega-Weekes, 'The Churchwardens' Accounts of South Tawton', *Transactions of the Devonshire Association*, Vol. 39, 1907, 318-319.

159 Devon Record Office, Diocesan Faculty Petitions, Atherington.

160 Devon Record Office, CC181/9, 11.

161 Devon Record Office, Principal Registry, Basket A/1691.

162 Devon Record Office, Diocesan Faculty Causes, Cornwood, 1699.

163 Devon Record Office, Principal Registry, Basket A/1752, North Petherwin & Honiton.

164 Devon Record Office, Principal Registry, Basket A/1827.

165 Devon Record Office, Principal Registry 517/191 (Sidbury).

166 Devon Record Office, Principal Registry, Basket A/1827.

167 Devon Record Office, Diocesan Faculty Causes, Cornwood, 1699; Devon Record Office, Principal Registry, 517/168 (Pinhoe).

168 Devon Record Office, CC181, Ashprington.

169 Devon Record Office, Principal Registry, Basket A/1682.

170 Devon Record Office, Diocesan Faculty Causes, Exmouth.

171 Devon Record Office, Diocesan Faculty Causes, Whitestone; Principal Registry, Basket A/1667. See also 3459M/F14 for Whitestone.

172 Devon Record Office, CC41/181 & CC91/44.

173 Devon Record Office, CC4A/86.

174 Devon Record Office, 2749A/P1/2/6/1.

175 Devon Record Office, Principal Registry, 517/60 (Colebrooke); Westcountry Studies Library, sB/COL 5/1618/MOR, Percy Morris (ed.), Colebrooke churchwardens' accounts, 17-18.

176 Devon Record Office, Principal Registry, 517/144-5 (Milton Abbot).

177 Devon Record Office, CC181, Ashwater. It was still being planned in 1788: Devon Record Office, Diocesan Faculty Petitions, Ashwater, 1788.

178 Devon Record Office, Diocesan Faculty Causes, Hatherleigh.

179 Devon Record Office, Diocesan Faculty Causes, Iddesleigh.

180 Devon Record Office, Principal Registry, 3264/6/29.

181 Devon Record Office, 2935A-99/PW1.

182 Whiting, *Blind Devotion*, 193.

183 Chanter, *The Church of St Brannock*, 8.

184 Devon Record Office, Consistory Court, church rate of St Dominic, 10 March 1630/1.

185 Devon Record Office, CC22/96.

186 Devon Record Office, CC6A/68.

187 North Devon Record Office, 1201A/PW8-10; Devon Record Office, CC91/120. The case refers to the date 1616.

188 North Devon Record Office, 1201A/PW8-10 & 1843A/PW130.

189 Devon Record Office, Diocesan Faculty Causes, North Tawton.

190 Devon Record Office, Principal Registry, 517/108 (High Bray).

191 Devon Record Office, Principal Registry, 517/161 (Okehampton) & CC19/127.

192 Devon Record Office, Diocesan Faculty Causes, Chulmleigh.

193 Devon Record Office, Diocesan Faculty Causes, Honiton, 1765.

194 Devon Record Office, 180A/PR/1/6.

195 William J. Woolcombe, 'Hat pegs in churches', *Devon & Cornwall Notes & Queries*, Volume 11, Part 1, 1920, 38-9.

196 John Agate, *Benches and Stalls in Suffolk Churches* (Suffolk Historic Churches Trust, 1980), 16. Wellow in Somerset have benches similar to Atherington: Howard & Crossley, *English Church Woodwork*, 307-8.

197 Devon Record Office, Z19/21/6. The seat was in the church when Davidson visited in 1843: Westcountry Studies Library, s726.5/DEV/DAV U, 153.

198 Sabine Baring Gould, *A Book of the West* (1900), 152-3.

199 A handful of plain ancient seats can also be seen in the west end of the church.

200 The benches have been in the north transept since Davidson saw them on 20 October 1846: Westcountry Studies Library, s726.5/DEV/DAV U, Church Notes [in the] South of Devon, 377.

201 The Royal Albert Memorial Museum's collection of objects collected by Harry Hems has fragments of bench ends with poppy heads from Bere Ferrers.

202 Devon Record Office, 1070.

203 John Wallis, *The Bodmin Register* (Bodmin, 1830), 33-5.

204 North Devon Record Office, 1843A/PW61.

205 In 1892 it was noted by T. N. Brushfield that the seats at Colaton Raleigh were plain: T. N. Brushfield, 'The Church of All Saints, East Budleigh', *Transactions of the Devonshire Association*, Vol. 24, 1892, 222.

206 Two others are in Braunton. These have corners which had designs scratched into them but they were left unfinished in order to fix something (as yet undetermined) on them.

207 Howard and Crossley, *English Church Woodwork*, 305.

208 Beatrix F. Cresswell, 'Sittings in Church', *Devon & Cornwall Notes & Queries*, Volume 9, Part 4, October 1916, 118.

209 Devon Record Office, 462A/PW/1/1/1. The churchwardens' accounts begin this year and it may be that the remaining seats had been built sometime previously for when there are no surviving documents. Only seven shillings and seventeen pennies were given to Mr Shenton and his mate for building seats and another three shillings subsequently. Four years later a joiner was paid for 2½ days' work on seating. Another seat was erected the following year.

210 Westcountry Studies Library, rough notes, sx726.5/WES/EXE.

211 W. P. S., 'Nooks and Corners of Devon', *Exeter Flying Post*, 20 July 1848.

212 Later Cornish bench ends with paint can be seen at Lanreath, Lanteglos and Talland. Paint was applied to early bench ends at St Breward but this may have been done later.

213 John Riddington Young, *Saint Michael's Church Horwood* (Horwood, 2001), 19.

214 *The Church of the Holy Trinity, Weare Giffard* (Weare Giffard, no date given).

215 Smith, *Church Woodcarvings*, 85. Alwington also has letters upside down.

216 G. O. Apthorp, 'The Church of St Mary the Virgin, Rewe', *Transactions of the Exeter Diocesan Architectural Society*, 3rd Series, Vol. 3, 1912, 120-3.

217 Howard and Crossley, *English Church Woodwork*, 305; Nikolaus Pevsner, *Cornwall* (1951), 21.

218 *St Swithun's Church Sandford; A Guide For Visitors & Pilgrims* (Sandford) no page number; *Parish Church of Saint Mary & Saint Gregory, Frithelstock* (Frithelstock), no page number; M. G. Challis, *Life in Medieval England as portrayed on church misericords and bench ends* (Nettlebed, 1997), 14; H. C. Geipel, *St Thomas of Canterbury, Northlew* (Northlew, 1997 edn), 6.

219 Allen T. Hussell, *North Devon Churches* (Barnstaple, 1909), 20.

220 T. N. Brushfield, 'The Church of All Saints, East Budleigh', *Transactions of the Devonshire Association*, Vol. 25, 1893, 291.

221 Smith, *Church Woodcarvings*, 67.

222 *Notes on the parish church of St Peter and St Paul Churchstanton* (Churchstanton, no date or page numbers given).

223 Westcountry Studies Library, s726.5/DEV/DAVU, Church Notes [in the] West of Devon, 361.

224 Devon Record Office, Principal Registry, 517/147.

225 These are Ashcombe, Ashton, Atherington, Bere Ferrers, Bickleigh, Broadhempston, Buckland Monachorum, Cheriton Bishop, Christow, Chudleigh, Coldridge, Colebrooke, Dartington, Drewesteignton, Dunchideock, East Ogwell, Kenn, Kingston, Modbury, Plymtree, South Tawton, Stoke Gabriel, Talaton, Tedburn St Mary and Whimple. Powderham has one bench end which does not have blank tracery. Cockington's carving combines Gothic tracery with linen-fold. Bench ends held by the Royal Albert Memorial Museum for the churches of Clyst St George and Staverton also have tracery.

226 Rame and Sheviock, both on the Rame Peninsula, in the south-east tip of Cornwall, have blank tracery but the other churches in East Cornwall with ancient bench-ends have more elaborate carving. Lawhitton near Launceston has blank shields placed within its tracery.

227 Harold Tucker, *The Parish Church of The Holy Cross Tetcott* (Tetcott, 1994), 6.

228 Sidney W. Cornish, *Short Notes on the church and parish of Ottery St Mary, Devon* (Exeter, 1869), 7-8.

229 E. K. Prideaux, 'Examples of Renaissance Church Woodwork in Devon', *Devon & Cornwall Notes & Queries*, Volume 5, Part 3, July 1910, 66.

230 E. K. Prideaux, 'Sutcombe Church and its Builders', *Devon & Cornwall Notes & Queries*, Volume 8, 1915, appendix, 30.

231 Francis Bond, *Wood Carvings in English Churches: 1*, Misericords (Oxford, 1910), preface.

232 Beatrix Cresswell, 'Hinkypunk', *Devon & Cornwall Notes & Queries*, Volume 15, Part 3, July 1928, 109-110.

233 *All Saints Church and the village of East Budleigh* (East Budleigh, 2010), 20. The listing buildings survey notes the bench end as 'a very early representation of a North American native' but in 1978 an earlier parish guide recognised it as a Green Man: *All Saints East Budleigh* (1978, East Budleigh), 25.

234 Todd Gray, *Devon's Fifty Best Churches* (Exeter, 2011), 33-5.

235 English Heritage, Listed Building Survey; *A guide to St Mary's, the parish church of Bideford* (Bideford, no date given).

236 Westcountry Studies Library, s726.5/DEV/DAV U, Church Notes [in the] West of Devon, 5.

237 The few at Dolton and Huntsham also avoid Gothic tracery.

238 E. K. Prideaux, *Examples of Renaissance Church Woodwork in Devon*, *Devon & Cornwall Notes & Queries*, Volume 5, Part 3, July 1910, 66.

239 Todd Gray, *Lost Devon* (Exeter, 2003), 68-70.

240 Westcountry Studies Library, s726.5/DEV/DAV U, Church Notes [in the] South of Devon, 861.

241 Nigel Morgan, 'The Monograms, Arms and Badges of the Virgin Mary in Late Medieval England', in John Cherry and Ann Payne (eds) *Signs and Symbols*, Harlaxton Medieval Studies, XVIII (Donington, 2009), 57.

242 Wright, *The Rural Benchends of Somerset*, 78-9. These three are at Kingston St Mary and Cheddar. A fourth is at Milverton.

243 J. Brooking Rowe, *A History of the borough of Plympton Erle* (Exeter, 1906), 236.

244 *Combeinteignhead Parish Church; an architectural and historical description* (Combeinteignhead, no date given); J. M. Slader, *The Churches of Devon* (Newton Abbot, 1968), 94; Smith, Church Woodcarvings, 21, 45.

245 Powderham Castle has a carving of what is probably St Paul.

246 A mid nineteenth-century drawing in the collection of the Exeter Diocesan Architectural Society shows the bench end without the head of Christ. Close examination of the carving shows careful restoration. Various writers have failed to notice the repair including J. C. D. Smith in *A guide to Church Woodcarvings*, 21.

247 Westcountry Studies Library, sx726.5/WES/EXE.

248 Abbotsham, Ashwater, Braunton, Broadwoodwidger, Dowland, Down St Mary, Frithelstock, George Nympton, Hartland, High Bickington, Horwood, Lapford, Lewtrenchard, Marwood, Monkleigh, Mortehoe, Newton St Petrock, Northlew, St Giles on the Heath, Sutcombe, Welcombe, Westleigh and West Woolfardisworthy.

249 Eamon Duffy, *The Stripping of the Altars* (Yale, 2005), 234-48.

250 Marwood also has pincers upside down on a shield.

251 These are Thorncombe, Bradford Abbas, Nether Compton, Leigh, Leweston, Folke, Fordington, Yet Minster and Hillfield.

252 J. F. Chanter, *The Church of St Brannock, Braunton* (Braunton, 1909, reprint 2009), 8.

253 The question to what extent Cornwall had its own identity has been most recently discussed by Mark Stoyle in West Britons: *Cornish Identities and the Early Modern British State* (Exeter, 2002).

254 Todd Gray (ed.), *The Chronicle of Exeter, 1205 - 1722* (Exeter, 2005), 81-2.

255 Whiting, *Blind Devotion*, 126,

256 Whiting, *Blind Devotion*, 144.

257 Frances Rose-Troup, *The Western Rebellion of 1549* (1913), 180-3; Whiting, *Blind Devotion*, 129-30; Devon Record Office, CC91/4.

258 Gray, *Lost Devon*, 155.

259 Robert Whiting, *The Reformation of the English Parish Church* (Cambridge, 2010), 3-20.

260 'Proceedings held at the 56th annual meeting held at Barnstaple', 24th to 26th July 1917, *Transactions of the Devonshire Association*, Vol. 49, 1917, 20.

261 Todd Gray (ed.), *The Lost Chronicle of Barnstaple, 1586 - 1611* (Exeter, 1998), 62.

262 Todd Gray, 'Devon's Fisheries and Early Stuart Northern New England', in Michael Duffy, Stephen Fisher, David J. Starkey and Joyce Youings (eds), *The New Maritime History of Devon* (1992), 139-44.

263 David Loades, 'Sir Richard Grenville', *Oxford Dictionary of National Biography*.

264 Audrey Erskine, Vyvyan Hope and John Lloyd, *Exeter Cathedral* (Exeter, 1988), 53-5.

265 Mark McDermott, 'Early Bench ends in All Saints' Church, Trull', *Proceedings of the Somerset Archaeology and Natural History Society*, 138 (1994), 118-120; Katharine French, *The People of the Parish* (Philadelphia, 2011), 163.

266 The view that the jar is an aspersorium has been held by several writers: Smith, *Church Woodcarvings*, 31, disagreed with it being a pestle and mortar while Wright, *The Rural Benchends of Somerset*, 79, 81 was also of the opinion it was an aspersorium. Penny Hebgin-Barnes in *The Medieval Stained Glass of Lancashire* (Oxford, 2009) believes a similar image represents pestles and mortar perhaps for the mixing of spices for entombing.

267 A somewhat similar motif can be seen at High Bickington.

268 The lines of blood were inserted into the Doddiscombsleigh window during the Victorian restoration and may have been based on a similar window at Cadbury in which only the central figure has survived.

269 Whiting, *Blind Devotion*, 70, 168, 222.

270 Westcountry Studies Library, sx726.5/WES/EXE.

271 Hanham, *Churchwardens' Accounts of Ashburton*, 41; Wallis, *The Bodmin Register*, 33-5.

272 Hobbs, *St Nectan's*, 185.

273 W. G. Hoskins, *Devon* (1954), 271-2.

274 T. L. Stoate (ed.), *Devon Lay Subsidy Rolls 1524-7* (1979), 94-5, 92.

275 North Devon Record Office, 1677A/PW1A, the entry for 1583 notes 'for carriage of the same seats from Barnstaple 12d'.

276 Devon Record Office, Principal Registry, Basket A/1696.

277 *Francis Bond, Screens and Galleries in English Churches* (1908), 56, 86-90; John Allan, 'Immigrant Craftsmen in South-West England, 1500-1600', *Post-Medieval Archaeology, forthcoming*.

278 Allan, 'Immigrant Craftsmen', forthcoming.

279 Plymouth & West Devon Record Office, 1272, folio 61v. Martin was a common name in the South Hams but there was an alien with the name Thomas Martin in Plymouth in the 1520s: T. L. Stoate (ed.), *Devon Lay Subsidy Rolls 1524-7* (1979), 157.

280 Soate, *Devon Lay Subsidy Rolls*,141.

281 John Paris was listed in the 1524 subsidy roll but not as a foreigner: Stoate, *Devon Lay Subsidy Rolls*, 141.

282 Francis Mardon Osborne (ed.), *The Church Wardens' Accounts of St Michael's Church, Chagford, 1480 – 1600* (Chagford, 1979), 94.

283 Ivon L. Gregory (ed.), *Hartland Church Accounts, 1597-1706* (Frome, 1950), 61.

284 Osborne, *Chagford*, 76.

285 Devon Record Office, 482A/PW21. There were also payments that year to 'Robert the carpenter' who appears to have lived at Buckland Monachorum. That year another carpenter by the name of Collyns was also paid and he worked on the seats in subsequent years. In 1588 the carpenter was Walter Burges; Plymouth & West Devon Record Office, 1/132, folio 18v. I am grateful to Professor Mark Brayshay for this reference. These could have been for the guildhall although it is more likely that 'seat' would have been used in preference to 'pew'. In 1609 William Scoble, joiner, of Plymouth, had a lease on a house in Southside Street: Plymouth & West Devon Record Office, 1/425/47.

286 J. F. Chanter, *The Church of St Brannock*, Braunton (Braunton, 1909, reprint 2009), 8.

287 Westcountry Studies Library, Devon & Cornwall Record Society Library, transcript of Winkleigh churchwardens' account, 37; Devon Record Office, Principal Registry 517/97.

288 Possibly the first, and only, discussion of punch marks in relation to Devon bench ends was made by T. N. Brushfield for East Budleigh: T. N. Brushfield, 'The Church of All Saints, East Budleigh', *Transactions of the Devonshire Association*, Vol. 24, 1892, 222.

289 These are in the vestry and not in the main body of the church.

290 Westcountry Studies Library, SPh/P&D 08264.

291 Bench end panels that were reused in the pulpit at Week St Mary, near the border with Devon, also have this decoration. West Worlington and Cockington also have bench ends with linen-fold panelling.

292 Devon Record Office, Z19/21/6, pages 192, 194; H. Tapley Soper, 'Heraldry in Bridford Church', *Devon & Cornwall Notes & Queries*, Volume 8, Part 3, July 1914, 73-6. The chair was built before 1843.

293 Hobbs, *Hartland*, 253, 234. There are four in total.

294 Tara Hamling, *Decorating the 'Godly' Household* (New Haven and London, 2010), 269-71.

295 I am grateful to Reverend Richard Dorrington for this information.

296 Mattingly, 'Bench Ends', 8; I am grateful to Emeritus Professor Christopher Holdsworth for this translation. The text is probably delivered from Psalm 102 verse 17 (Vulgate).

Illustration sources

All photographs by the author with the exceptions of page 11, *A True Relation of Those Sad and Lamentable Accidents Which Happened In and About the Parish Church of Withycombe in the Dartmoores in Devonshire on Sunday the 21 of October last 1638*; page 23, 52 Westcountry Studies Library (hereafter WSL), SC1895; page 27, North Devon Record Office (hereafter NDRO), Braunton 1677A/PW1A; page 44-5, Devon Record Office (hereafter DRO), DD61409; page 51, North Devon Athenaeum, Hardy Mss; WSL, page 52, SC0302; page 60 WSL, Harry Hems Scrapbooks; pages 64 & 65 Plymouth & West Devon Record Office, 116/36, for which attempts have been made to find the owner of the copyright of the image; pages 70-1, DRO, Chanter 733; page 72, DRO, Chanter 733; page 73, DRO, Chanter 733; page 75, WSL, SC2469 & bottom SC0534; page 76, DRO, Faculty Causes, Wembury & Principal Registry, 517/168; page 78, DRO, CC4a/52; page 79, *Express & Echo*; page 81, NDRO, 1843a/pw130; page 82, DRO, CC91/120; page 88, WSL, P&D00406; page 105 left, North Devon Athenaeum, Hardy Mss; page 118, Devon & Exeter Institution (hereafter DEI), Exeter Diocesan Architectural Society Scrapbook; page 150, middle, DEI, Exeter Diocesan Architectural Society Scrapbook; page 158, private collection; page 168, DEI, Exeter Diocesan Architectural Society Scrapbook; page 170, top, WSL, Harry Hems Scrapbooks, bottom, *Devonshire Association Transactions*, volume 24, 1892, plate 6; page 171, WSL, P&D08264; Joseph Moxon, *Mechanick Exercises* (1703). The images located in the stated institutions have been reproduced with their copyright permission.

Ashcombe.

Index